SARAH MELLAND

THE
ART OF WAR
& DATING

ISBN:
Paperback: 978-1-969137-20-4
Hardcover: 978-1-969137-21-1

Printed in the United States of America
First Edition

Table of Contents

INTRODUCTION

Why *The Art of War* Belongs in Dating

Modern dating doesn't fail because women don't care enough. It fails because they care without strategy.

We were taught to be open, patient, intuitive, communicative, forgiving. We were not taught how to observe, verify, time our moves, or exit cleanly when reality doesn't match potential.

So, we stay too long.
We explain too much.
We bleed slowly instead of deciding early.

Sun Tzu wrote *The Art of War* for one purpose: to end conflict efficiently, with minimal loss.

That's the entire point of this book.

This is not about manipulation.
It's not about power games.
It's not about "winning" men.

It's about self-command.

Dating is not romance in the abstract. It's decision-making under uncertainty. You are constantly assessing terrain, signals, timing, risk, and cost. When you ignore those

1

elements, you don't become more loving, you become more exposed.

Strategy doesn't make you cold. It makes you clear.

This book translates Sun Tzu's principles into dating because the patterns are the same:
- confusion thrives where information is ignored
- chaos grows where boundaries are vague
- wars drag on when exits aren't planned
- losses compound when decisions are emotional

And most importantly: peace comes from ending the wrong battles early.

You do not read this book to stay in war mode.
You read it so you don't have to.

The women who move through dating with ease aren't harder. They see sooner. They act cleaner. They leave once.

This book is for women who are done guessing.
Done romanticizing inconsistency.
Done calling anxiety "chemistry."
Done confusing patience with self-sacrifice.

You don't need to try harder.
You need to see clearly.

That's what strategy gives you. And once you have it, you can finally put the armor down.

HOW TO USE THIS BOOK

(AND NOT USE IT AGAINST YOURSELF)

This book is not a checklist. It's a lens. You don't apply every principle at once. You don't "test" men. You don't manufacture scenarios to see how someone reacts. Strategy is responsive, not performative.

You observe first. You gather information.
You let patterns reveal themselves.

This book is meant to reduce confusion, not create paranoia. If you find yourself hyper-analyzing every text, rereading every interaction, or trying to "catch" someone, stop. That's not strategy. That's anxiety wearing tactical clothing.

Use this book when:
- something feels off
- effort and outcome don't match
- boundaries create chaos instead of clarity
- you're tempted to explain instead of decide

Do not use this book to:
- withhold as punishment
- perform indifference
- control outcomes
- override your own nervous system

If you are dysregulated, attached to a specific result, or afraid to lose him, pause. Strategy only works when you are willing to accept either outcome.

The goal is not to stay guarded forever. The goal is to see clearly early so you don't need armor later.

Most women don't fail at dating because they lack intuition. They fail because they ignore what they already know.

This book exists to help you stop doing that.

Read slowly.
Apply selectively.
Exit cleanly.

And remember: the most strategic move is knowing when you're done thinking.

SELF COMMAND BEFORE STRATEGY

No strategy works when you're dysregulated.

You cannot time a move while flooded.
You cannot read patterns while anxious.
You cannot decide cleanly when you're attached to a specific outcome.

Before Sun Tzu ever talks about terrain or attack, he assumes command is stable. That's the part most people skip and why strategy fails them.

Self-command means you can:
- tolerate discomfort without reacting
- sit with uncertainty without chasing clarity
- let silence exist without filling it
- allow an outcome you don't prefer

If you can't do those things yet, that's not a flaw. It just means you don't move *now*.

This chapter is not telling you to suppress emotion.
It's telling you to regulate before you act.

There is a difference. Emotion gives information. Dysregulation distorts it.

If you're spiraling, bargaining, fantasizing, or rehearsing speeches in your head, pause. No boundary set from panic holds. No exit made from fear feels clean.

Self-command looks unglamorous:

- sleep
- eat
- move your body
- talk to someone grounded
- wait one full nervous system cycle before acting

You are not losing ground by stabilizing.
You are securing it.

Only when your body is calm does strategy become visible. Timing sharpens. Choices simplify. The right move becomes obvious not because it's dramatic, but because it's quiet.

Strategy is not about force.
It's about clarity under pressure.

And clarity belongs to the woman who can command herself first.

MISAPPLIED STRATEGY

(How Women Turn Tools Into Self-Harm)

Strategy only works when it's used to protect reality, not override it.

When applied from fear, strategy mutates. It stops being discernment and starts becoming self-abandonment dressed up as control. This is where women go wrong.

When Strategy Becomes Performance
Silence is meant to create clarity. But when silence is used to provoke, punish, or test, it becomes a performance. If you're withholding to see if he notices, that's not strategy. That's hope wearing armor.

When Boundaries Become Ultimatums
A boundary is something *you* enforce. An ultimatum is something you threaten hoping he'll change. If the boundary only exists if he complies, you don't have a boundary, you have a negotiation you're afraid to lose.

When Observation Turns Into Surveillance
Gathering information means watching what happens naturally. It does **not** mean obsessing, tracking, rereading, or decoding. If your "strategy" increases anxiety instead of reducing it, you've left intelligence and entered fixation.

When Detachment Becomes Dissociation

Pulling back is meant to restore balance. But if you're numbing yourself to stay, minimizing your needs, or convincing yourself you "don't care" when you do, that's not strength. That's dissociation.

When Strategy Is Used to Get Picked

This is the most dangerous misuse. If you're applying principles to appear unbothered, more desirable, or harder to lose, you've flipped the purpose. Strategy is not for earning commitment. It's for deciding if commitment is warranted.

The Litmus Test

Ask yourself this one question: Is this move protecting me or protecting the fantasy?

If it protects the fantasy, stop.
If it protects your future, proceed.

Real strategy simplifies.
It doesn't contort you.

You should feel clearer, calmer, and more grounded not tighter, quieter, or smaller.

Tools are meant to be set down once they've done their job. If you're bleeding while holding them, you're using them wrong.

This book is here to help you stop hurting yourself *beautifully* and start choosing yourself cleanly.

THE DATING UNEXPERT PEPTALK

(The Human Reminder)

Let me say this plainly:

You're not bad at dating.
You're not too much.
You're not "doing it wrong."

You just stayed longer than the situation deserved.

Most women don't need more advice. They need permission to stop doubting what they already see. You didn't imagine the shift. You didn't misread the inconsistency. You didn't ask for too much, you asked the wrong person for it.

This book might feel sharp at times. That's intentional. Not to harden you, but to cut through the noise that kept you stuck.

If you're reading this with a lump in your throat, good. That means you're waking up. If you're feeling relief instead of heartbreak, even better. That means you're finally telling yourself the truth without cruelty.

Here's what I want you to remember:
- You are allowed to leave without a dramatic reason.

- You are allowed to change your mind once new information appears.
- You are allowed to protect your peace even if no one did anything "that bad."

Closure is not something someone gives you. It's something you grant yourself when you stop negotiating with reality.

You don't need to confront perfectly.
You don't need to explain clearly.
You don't need to be understood.
You need to be done.

Strategy is not about becoming colder. It's about becoming cleaner. And clean exits don't haunt you, they free you.

If you take nothing else from this book, take this:
- You were never asking for too much.
- You were asking the wrong terrain to support you.

And once you see that, you stop blaming yourself and you move on with dignity intact.

I promise you this: The moment you stop abandoning yourself, dating gets quieter. Easier. Less dramatic. Not because people change, but because *you* do.

And that's not losing softness.
That's growing a spine.

I'm on your side.
Always.

CHAPTER 1

LAYING PLANS
The First Date Is Not a Vibe Check

Sun Tzu said the art of war is of vital importance to the State. Dating is of vital importance to your sanity. This is not dramatic. This is logistics.

Who you let into your life determines your emotional economy, your sleep schedule, your self-esteem, and how often you find yourself staring at your phone wondering why a grown man has suddenly "needed space" since Tuesday.

Dating is a matter of life and death. Not literal death. Emotional death. Dignity death. The slow erosion of self-respect that happens when you ignore patterns and call it chemistry.

Which is why the first date is not a vibe check. It is reconnaissance.

If you treat it like vibes, you end up surprised. If you treat it like strategy, you end up safe.

THE FIVE CONSTANT FACTORS
(A.K.A. WHY YOU KEEP LOSING)

Sun Tzu says every battle is governed by five constant factors. Dating is no different. Ignore them, and you lose before the appetizers arrive.

1. The Moral Law

(Alignment. Not attraction.)

"The Moral Law causes the people to be in complete accord with their ruler, so that they will follow him regardless of their lives, undismayed by any danger."

- Sun Tzu

The Moral Law is not whether you *like* him. It's whether your values, intentions, and emotional pace are in alignment.

Does he want the same outcome you want or is he just enjoying the attention while he figures his life out on your time?

Men will follow a ruler they believe in. You should only entertain a man who is clear about where he is going.

Confusion is not depth.
Ambiguity is not romance.
And potential is not a plan.

If you are not in moral alignment, nothing else matters.

2. Heaven

(Timing. Energy. Seasons.)

"Heaven signifies night and day, cold and heat, times and seasons."

- Sun Tzu

Translation:
Just because he's charming doesn't mean he's *available*.
Just because he's available doesn't mean he's *ready*.
And just because he's ready doesn't mean he's ready for you.

A man in the wrong season will burn everything he touches and blame the weather.

If his life is chaos, his dating will be chaos.
He is not "going through something."
He *is* something.

3. Earth

(Terrain. Environment. Reality.)

"Earth comprises distances, great and small; danger and security; open ground and narrow passes; the chances of life and death."

- Sun Tzu

Dating terrain matters more than people want to admit. Dating apps are hostile territory. Late-night first dates are narrow passes. "Let's just see where it goes" is a cliff.

Where did he choose to meet you? How much effort did it require? Was there an exit strategy or was it designed to linger?

A man who puts you in compromised terrain early is not romantic. He is efficient for himself.

4. The Commander

(Leadership. Character. Backbone.)

The Commander stands for the virtues of wisdom, sincerity, benevolence, courage and strictness.

- Sun Tzu

Translation: Does he lead his own life or is he improvising every decision? Is he honest even when it's inconvenient? Does he follow through? Can he make a plan without crowdsourcing his masculinity?

A weak commander blames circumstances. A strong one takes responsibility. You are not looking for perfection. You are looking for *command presence*.

5. Method and Discipline

(Consistency. Structure. Behavior.)

Method and discipline are systems: how things are organized, enforced, and maintained. This is where women lie to themselves.

Does he text consistently or in emotional bursts?
Does he make plans or just suggestions?
Are his actions disciplined, or reactive?

Chemistry without discipline is chaos.
Romance without structure is a liability.

THE SEVEN CALCULATIONS
(THE ONES YOU KEEP SKIPPING)

Sun Tzu says victory can be predicted before the battle begins.
Dating is no different.
Ask yourself:

1. Who is more emotionally aligned, you or him?
2. Who has more self-awareness?
3. Who benefits more from the current setup?
4. Who enforces boundaries consistently?
5. Who has more leverage?
6. Who has done the work?
7. Who rewards good behavior and removes access for bad behavior?

If the answer is always *him*, congratulations, you're volunteering.

ADAPTABILITY IS NOT DESPERATION

"According as circumstances are favorable, one should modify one's plans."

- Sun Tzu

Sun Tzu warns against rigid plans.
Translation: You don't double down when information changes.
If new data arrives inconsistency, defensiveness, confusion, you adapt.

You do not argue with reality. You do not negotiate attraction. You do not chase clarity from someone benefiting from your confusion. That's not flexibility. That's self-abandonment.

ALL DATING IS BASED ON DECEPTION

"All warfare is based on deception."

- Sun Tzu

Sun Tzu said it. I didn't. People perform on first dates. Men included. They show you who they want to be, not who they are under pressure.

This is why you don't overshare. This is why you don't reveal your emotional arsenal. This is why you don't audition for intimacy. Mystery is not manipulation. It's pacing.

CONTROL THE PERCEPTION, CONTROL THE POWER

"When able to attack, we must seem unable; when using our forces, we must seem inactive; when we are near, we must make the enemy believe we are far away; when far away, we must make him believe we are near."

- Sun Tzu

When you're interested, don't announce it.
When you're available, don't broadcast it.
When you're close, don't rush intimacy.
When you pull back, don't explain yourself.

Dating strategy isn't about deception, it's about discipline. The person who controls how much is revealed, when, and why holds the advantage. Mystery creates focus. Restraint creates curiosity. And curiosity is what makes someone lean in instead of lean away. Power begins the moment you stop over-signaling.

FEIGN NOTHING. OBSERVE EVERYTHING.

"Hold out baits to entice the enemy. Feign disorder, and crush him."

- Sun Tzu

If he is arrogant, let him talk. If he is inconsistent, let him show you. If he is lazy, do not rescue him. You don't expose a man.

15

You let him expose himself. The fastest way to lose is to correct behavior before it's revealed.

NEVER FIGHT THE FORTIFIED EGO

"If he is secure at all points, be prepared for him. If he is in superior strength, evade him."

- Sun Tzu

If he seems unshakeable, overconfident, or "good on paper," don't rush in swinging. Strength that looks solid is often just well-defended insecurity. When someone presents as emotionally fortified, your job isn't to break through. It's to observe, reposition, and wait.

And if he holds more power than you: status, attention, options, emotional detachment, don't try to overpower him. Evade. Preserve your energy. Let the imbalance reveal itself naturally.

Strategy isn't confrontation.
Strategy is knowing when *not* to engage.

Winning doesn't come from fighting the strongest version of someone. It comes from refusing to play a rigged game.

TRIGGER THE EGO, NOT THE WAR

"If your opponent is of choleric temper, seek to irritate him. Pretend to be weak, that he may grow arrogant."

- Sun Tzu

If someone is hot-tempered, reactive, or easily offended, you don't need to confront them. You need to let them unravel themselves. A volatile ego is already halfway to defeat.

Appearing calm, soft, or even underestimated invites arrogance. And arrogance creates mistakes. When someone believes they have the upper hand, they stop masking who they are.

You don't win by overpowering emotion. You win by letting it expose itself.

Let them overplay. Let them talk too much. Let them show their hand. True power isn't loud. It's composed, strategic, and always one move ahead.

DISRUPT HIS COMFORT

"If he is taking his ease, give him no rest. If his forces are united, separate them."
- Sun Tzu

Comfort breeds complacency. When someone is relaxed, unchallenged, and certain of your availability, they stop investing, because nothing is at stake.

Your job isn't to nag or demand attention.
Your job is to *remove the guarantee.*

Change the rhythm. Pull back your energy. Stop being predictable. When ease disappears, effort reappears.

Momentum in dating doesn't come from chasing, it comes from contrast. The moment someone has to *adjust* to you, they reveal how much they actually value you.

Peace is earned. Access is earned. And attention should never be assumed. Stay just elusive enough to matter.

UNPREDICTABLE PRESENCE

"Attack him where he is unprepared, appear where you are not expected."
- Sun Tzu

People defend what they can anticipate. They relax around patterns. They armor up only where they expect impact. So don't fight on familiar ground.

17

Show confidence where they assumed insecurity. Pull away where they expected pursuit. Speak plainly where they thought you'd stay silent.

The power move isn't confrontation, it's *disruption*.

When you appear differently than expected, you bypass defenses entirely. You're no longer reacting to their behavior; you're rewriting the dynamic.

Surprise shifts leverage. Uncertainty creates attention. And the moment they have to *recalculate you*, you're already ahead. Be impossible to game. That's how strategy wins.

STRATEGIC SILENCE

"These military devices, leading to victory, must not be divulged beforehand."

- Sun Tzu

Power loses its edge when it's announced.

Explaining your intentions invites interference.
Forecasting your moves gives others time to adjust.
Oversharing turns strategy into spectacle.

The strongest position is quiet certainty.

You don't need validation.
You don't need agreement.
You don't need witnesses to your preparation.

Move in silence. Let outcomes speak.

When results arrive without warning, they land harder and no one has time to undermine them.

Mystery isn't avoidance. It's protection.
And strategy revealed too early isn't strategy at all.

THE FIRST DATE IS NOT THE BATTLE

Sun Tzu says battles are won before they are fought.

The first date is not about chemistry.
It is about information.

If you walk in hoping, fantasizing, projecting, you are unarmed.

If you walk in observant, curious, and grounded, you already have the advantage.

Men respect women who do not rush access.
Not because they are cruel.
Because they are *rare*.

FINAL CALCULATION

The general who makes many calculations before the battle wins.
The one who relies on vibes loses.

If you stop treating first dates like auditions and start treating them like assessments, everything changes.

You are not trying to be chosen.
You are deciding who is allowed closer.

And that alone shifts the power.

CHAPTER 2

WAGING WAR
Why Situationships Are Expensive

Sun Tzu opens this chapter with logistics for a reason.

Before a single blade is drawn, before anyone bleeds, before anyone wins or loses, the general counts the cost.

Dating works the same way. Most women don't lose because the man was malicious. They lose because they never calculated the expense.

Situationships are not confusing. They are financially reckless, emotionally inflationary, and structurally designed to drain you while calling it "connection."

THE TRUE COST OF ENGAGEMENT

Sun Tzu describes armies of enormous size: chariots, soldiers, provisions, armor, entertainment, supplies, maintenance. He is not being poetic. He is saying this: *Every campaign consumes resources you do not get back.*

Dating a man who is unsure costs you:
- Time
- Focus
- Emotional energy
- Sexual access
- Opportunity

20

- Confidence
- Nervous system stability

None of that is free.

And yet women enter prolonged emotional engagements with no supply plan, no exit strategy, and no guarantee of return. That is not romance. That is bad accounting.

WHEN VICTORY IS DELAYED, EVERYTHING DULLS

Sun Tzu warns that when victory takes too long:

- Weapons dull
- Ardor fades
- Strength drains

Translation: When clarity is delayed, attraction decays. That spark you keep trying to "revive" didn't die mysteriously. It died of *overexposure without progression.*

Long, undefined emotional engagements blunt desire. Men get comfortable. Women get anxious. No one wins. A man who truly wants you does not let the campaign drag on.

PROTRACTED CAMPAIGNS BANKRUPT STATES

Sun Tzu is blunt: *There is no instance of a country having benefited from prolonged warfare.*

No woman has ever benefited from a prolonged situationship. The longer it goes:

- The more you invest
- The harder it is to leave
- The more you justify behavior you would've rejected early

By the time you admit it isn't working, you've already paid too much to walk away cleanly, so you stay. That's how sunk cost becomes emotional captivity.

OTHERS MOVE IN WHEN YOU ARE WEAK

Sun Tzu warns that when resources are depleted, *other chieftains arise*.

Translation: While you're busy emotionally financing a man who won't commit, someone else is enjoying the benefits of your absence.

Men don't compete when they sense availability without consequence. They wait. And when you finally leave exhausted, you don't reenter the dating pool energized. You limp back in resentful, guarded, and depleted.

That's not because dating is hard. It's because you fought the wrong war too long.

SPEED IS NOT CARELESSNESS. IT'S MERCY

Sun Tzu makes one of his most misunderstood points here:

Haste can be foolish. But delay is *always* costly.

Translation: You don't rush intimacy, but you also don't linger in ambiguity.

There is no cleverness in waiting years for someone to "figure it out."
There is no honor in patience without reciprocity.

Clarity is not pressure.
It is mercy.

ONLY THOSE WHO UNDERSTAND THE EVILS CAN DATE PROFITABLY

Sun Tzu says only those who understand the evils of war know how to conduct it well.

Women who have stayed too long know this truth viscerally.

They know:
- How much it costs to ignore intuition
- How expensive "hope" can be
- How exhausting it is to carry emotional labor alone

This is not bitterness. This is earned wisdom.

DO NOT RAISE A SECOND LEVY

Sun Tzu warns against repeatedly reinforcing a failing campaign.

Translation: Stop giving second chances to men who haven't earned the first. Stop explaining yourself again. Stop offering access in new forms. Stop lowering the bar to keep the connection alive. If the initial structure failed, reinvesting deeper will not save it.

BRING YOUR OWN SUPPLIES. FORAGE ELSEWHERE

Sun Tzu advises bringing your own resources and foraging on the enemy.

Dating translation (and this one matters): Bring your own fulfillment. Your own life. Your own joy.

Do not rely on one man to supply all emotional nourishment while offering nothing in return. If he cannot contribute meaningfully, you do not subsidize him.

DISTANCE MAKES EVERYTHING MORE EXPENSIVE

Sun Tzu explains that maintaining an army at a distance impoverishes the people.

Situationships are long-distance wars even when you live five miles apart.

You are always reaching. Always initiating. Always extending emotional supply lines. The farther clarity is, the more it costs you to sustain hope.

INFLATION HITS FIRST

Sun Tzu notes that wherever an army lingers, prices rise.

In dating, prolonged ambiguity inflates expectations without delivering value. Suddenly:
- You're overthinking texts
- You're negotiating crumbs
- You're emotionally taxed for basic decency

This is how standards erode quietly.

THE PEOPLE PAY FIRST

Sun Tzu is clear: the people suffer before the leaders do.

In dating, *you* are the people. The man keeps his freedom. You carry the stress. That imbalance is the tell.

A WISE GENERAL TAKES FROM THE ENEMY

Sun Tzu says victory comes from using the enemy's resources.

Dating translation: You do not chase investment, you *respond to it*.

24

You do not reward ambiguity. You reward clarity.
Effort is the currency. Consistency is the proof.

REWARDS CREATE MOMENTUM

Sun Tzu explains that soldiers fight better when rewarded.

Men pursue more decisively when effort is met with warmth not access. Affection is not a down payment. It's a response to demonstrated intent.

USE WHAT YOU CAPTURE OR WALK AWAY

Captured soldiers are treated kindly *and* repurposed.

Translation: If a man steps up, great. If he doesn't, you do not rehabilitate him. You exit. Not angrily. Not dramatically. Efficiently.

THE OBJECTIVE IS VICTORY NOT DURATION

Sun Tzu ends where he began: War is not about endurance. It's about resolution.

Dating is not about how long you can tolerate uncertainty. It's about whether the engagement improves your life. If it doesn't, it's already too expensive.

FINAL TRUTH

The leader determines whether the people live in peace or peril.

In dating, *you are the leader.*

If your love life feels exhausting, unclear, or draining, it's not because you're bad at love. It's because you stayed in a war that should have ended.

CHAPTER 3

ATTACK BY STRATAGEM
Never Chase What Can Be Lured

Sun Tzu opens with a correction most people miss. The goal of war is not destruction. It is preservation.

The highest victory is not burning the enemy's city to the ground. It is taking it intact.

Dating works the same way. If you leave scorched earth behind you every time — fights, emotional explosions, dramatic exits, long closure speeches — you are not winning.

You are surviving loudly. The most powerful outcomes leave everything intact: your dignity, your nervous system, your options, your future.

SUPREME EXCELLENCE REQUIRES NO FIGHTING

Sun Tzu says conquering every battle is not excellence. Breaking resistance without fighting is.

Translation: If you have to argue, convince, persuade, pressure, or perform for interest, you already lost.

Attraction that needs to be forced is not attraction.
Commitment that needs to be negotiated is not commitment.

The most successful women do not fight men into choosing them. They remove resistance by not supplying the chase. Men pursue clarity when access is not guaranteed.

BAULK THE PLAN, DON'T REACT TO IT

"Thus, the highest form of generalship is to baulk the enemy's plans; the next best is to prevent the junction of the enemy's forces; the next in order is to attack the enemy's army in the field; and the worst policy of all is to besiege walled cities."

-     Sun Tzu

Sun Tzu teaches that the highest strategy is to disrupt the enemy's plans before they unfold.

In dating, this means not reacting emotionally to behavior designed to test access.

- Pullbacks.
- Delays.
- Breadcrumbing.
- Sudden "busy" phases.

These are not random. They are probes. The woman who panics loses position. The woman who pauses changes the game. Silence is not weakness. It is counter-strategy.

ISOLATE THE FORCES

Sun Tzu says the next best move is preventing the enemy from joining forces.

Dating translation: Stop competing with his options. You do not need to know who else he's seeing. You do not need to win against imaginary women.

When you refuse to overextend, men lose the advantage of comparison. A woman who is unavailable for ambiguity forces decision.

FIELD BATTLES ARE LAST RESORTS

Sun Tzu ranks open combat below strategic positioning.

In dating, confrontation should be rare. If you are frequently "having talks," clarifying, resetting expectations, or revisiting the same issue, you are already besieging a city. And sieges are expensive.

NEVER BESIEGE WALLED CITIES

Sun Tzu is explicit: avoid sieges at all costs.

A walled city is a man who:
- Is emotionally defended
- Avoids vulnerability
- Deflects responsibility
- Delays clarity

You cannot storm this without casualties. Trying to break emotional walls through persistence is how women lose themselves. Time, energy, and self-respect are the price.

IRRITATION MAKES FOOLS OF GENERALS

"The general, unable to control his irritation, will launch his men to the assault like swarming ants with the result that one-third of his men are slain, while the town still remains untaken. Such are the disastrous effects of a siege."

- Sun Tzu

Sun Tzu warns against acting from impatience.

Dating translation: Never act from frustration. Frustration leads to:
- Ultimatums you don't enforce
- Over-explaining
- Emotional flooding

- "I just need to know where this is going"

The moment you act from irritation, you reveal need. And need collapses leverage.

SUBDUE WITHOUT BLOODSHED

"Therefore the skillful leader subdues the enemy's troops without any fighting; he captures their cities without laying siege to them; he overthrows their kingdom without lengthy operations in the field."

- Sun Tzu

The skilled leader wins without loss. Dating wins should not hurt.

If being with someone requires emotional self-harm, the strategy is wrong. When you stop chasing, stop correcting, stop persuading, the outcome resolves itself quickly. Either he steps forward or he disappears. Both are victories.

KEEP YOUR FORCES INTACT

"With his forces intact he will dispute the mastery of the Empire, and thus, without losing a man, his triumph will be complete."

- Sun Tzu

Sun Tzu emphasizes preserving strength. This means:

- Do not overinvest early
- Do not give emotional access without consistency
- Do not merge lives before clarity exists

Your energy is your army. Spend it deliberately.

NUMBERS MATTER, BUT SO DOES POSITION

Sun Tzu outlines when to surround, attack, divide, engage, or retreat.

Dating translation: If you have leverage, wait. If interest is equal, proceed. If you sense imbalance, slow down. If you are outmatched in investment, retreat.

Retreat is not failure. It is strategy. Staying when the odds are against you is not loyalty, it's ego.

SMALL FORCES LOSE THROUGH OBSTINACY

Sun Tzu warns that stubborn resistance against greater force ends in capture. In dating, this is staying attached to someone who holds all the power.

If he controls the pace, the labels, the access, and the outcome, you are already overextended. The only winning move is withdrawal.

THE GENERAL IS THE BULWARK

Sun Tzu says the strength of the State depends on the general.

In dating, you are the general. If your boundaries are inconsistent, your life becomes unstable. If your standards wobble, your confidence erodes. Strong leadership creates calm.

MISMANAGEMENT DESTROYS ARMIES

Sun Tzu outlines three leadership failures:

1. **Giving orders that cannot be followed**
   Translation: Expecting commitment from someone who has shown no capacity for it.
2. **Governing an army like a kingdom**
   Translation: Treating early dating like a relationship.
3. **Poor role assignment**
   Translation: Expecting emotional depth from someone who has never demonstrated it.

This creates chaos.

RESTLESS ARMIES COLLAPSE

"But when the army is restless and distrustful, trouble is sure to come from the other feudal princes. This is simply bringing anarchy into the army, and flinging victory away."

- Sun Tzu

When leadership is unclear, disorder follows.

Anxious attachment is not chemistry. It is disorder. And disorder always invites loss.

THE FIVE ESSENTIALS FOR VICTORY

Sun Tzu concludes with five truths:

1. Know when to advance and when to retreat
2. Handle both abundance and scarcity
3. Maintain internal alignment
4. Be prepared while others are not
5. Act without interference

Dating translation:

- Know when to lean in and when to step back
- Do not overvalue rare attention
- Stay aligned with yourself
- Let others reveal before you do
- Do not let fantasy override data

KNOW YOURSELF. KNOW THE ENEMY.

This is the core. If you know yourself but not the man, you will oscillate between hope and disappointment. If you know the man but not yourself, you will abandon your needs. If you know neither, you will repeat the pattern endlessly.

But if you know both? You stop chasing. You stop explaining. You stop fighting. And suddenly, the war ends. Without casualties.

31

CHAPTER 4

TACTICAL DISPOSITIONS
Don't Show Your Hand

Sun Tzu begins with a rule most people violate instinctively: The greatest fighters first make themselves impossible to defeat. Only then do they wait for the opportunity to win.

Dating fails when women reverse this order.

They look for chemistry before safety.
They look for excitement before stability.
They look for proof of desire before proof of character.

That is how defeat enters early and quietly.

DEFEAT IS PREVENTABLE. VICTORY IS INVITED.

Sun Tzu makes a distinction most people ignore: You can secure yourself against loss entirely on your own. You cannot force victory. Victory requires the other party to misstep.

Translation:
You do not *create* red flags.
You wait for them to appear.

Your job is not to convince someone to choose you. Your job is to not disqualify yourself while they reveal who they are.

CONCEALMENT IS PROTECTION

The skilled fighter secures himself through concealment.

In dating, this means:

- You do not reveal your full emotional landscape early
- You do not announce expectations before behavior supports them
- You do not disclose fears, wounds, or long-term desires to someone who has not earned context

This is not manipulation. It is containment.

Overexposure creates vulnerability without trust.

KNOWING HOW TO WIN IS NOT THE SAME AS WINNING

Sun Tzu says one may know how to conquer without being able to do it.

Dating translation: You can understand the patterns perfectly and still lose if you act prematurely. Knowledge without restraint is still defeat.

DEFENSE SIGNALS STRENGTH NOT FEAR

Sun Tzu states plainly: Defensive positioning is not weakness. It indicates sufficient strength to wait.

In dating, women are taught that slowing down means disinterest.

That is false.

Slowing down signals discernment.

When you do not rush intimacy, explanation, or emotional investment, you reveal surplus not scarcity.

HIDE DEEP. STRIKE CLEAN.

"The general who is skilled in defense hides in the most secret recesses of the earth; he who is skilled in attack flashes forth from the topmost heights of heaven. Thus on the one hand we have ability to protect ourselves; on the other, a victory that is complete."

- Sun Tzu

Sun Tzu's metaphors matter here. The skilled defender hides beneath the deepest earth. The skilled attacker strikes like lightning from the heavens.

Dating translation: Early on, you stay grounded, observant, and unrevealing. When the moment arrives: clarity, commitment, action, you respond decisively. No hesitation. No negotiation. Men respect certainty more than performance.

OBVIOUS WINS ARE NOT IMPRESSIVE

Sun Tzu says if the crowd can see the victory coming, it isn't excellence.

Dating translation: If everyone can see what you want, what you fear, and what you'll tolerate, you've lost leverage. The most effective women move quietly. They leave without speeches. They withdraw without drama. They accept effort without overpraising it. Their outcomes look "easy" because the work was invisible.

EFFORTLESS VICTORY IS THE GOAL

"What the ancients called a clever fighter is one who not only wins, but excels in winning with ease."

- Sun Tzu

Sun Tzu praises the one who wins with ease. Not intensity. Not struggle. Not endurance. Ease.

If dating feels heavy, it is poorly positioned. Effort should go toward *selection*, not *salvage*.

INVISIBLE VICTORIES EARN NO APPLAUSE

"Hence his victories bring him neither reputation for wisdom nor credit for courage."

- Sun Tzu

The best strategist gains no reputation for brilliance.

Because nothing exploded.
Nothing collapsed.
Nothing needed rescuing.

Dating wins should not be theatrical. If your friends don't know the details, you're probably doing it right.

MISTAKES ARE THE ONLY LOSSES

Sun Tzu says the clever fighter wins by making no mistakes.

Dating mistakes are almost always the same:
- Over-disclosure
- Over-investment
- Over-correction
- Over-patience

These are not kindnesses. They are breaches.
Mistakes create openings where none were required.

POSITION FIRST. ACTION SECOND.

Sun Tzu is precise: Victory is secured *before* the battle begins.

Dating translation: If you are already emotionally safe, aligned, and fulfilled, nothing someone does can destabilize you.

You are not chasing outcomes.
You are filtering candidates.

This reverses everything.

THE LOSING STRATEGIST FIGHTS FIRST

"…whereas he who is destined to defeat first fights and afterwards looks for victory."

- Sun Tzu

Those destined to lose jump into action and hope for victory later.

This looks like:

- Emotional escalation without commitment
- Sexual access without clarity
- Time investment without direction

Hope is not a strategy.

MORAL LAW + DISCIPLINE = CONTROL

Sun Tzu reintroduces moral law and discipline for a reason.

If you abandon your values to keep someone interested, you lose control.

If you bend boundaries to maintain momentum, you lose power.

Consistency is magnetic.

THE FIVE STEPS TO VICTORY
(YES, EVEN IN DATING)

Sun Tzu outlines the progression: Measurement, Estimation, Calculation, Balancing, Victory.

Dating translation: Measure behavior. Estimate consistency. Calculate effort over time. Balance investment.

Then, and only then, proceed. Skipping steps creates illusions.

MOMENTUM MAKES OUTCOMES INEVITABLE

"A victorious army opposed to a routed one, is as a pound's weight placed in the scale against a single grain."

- Sun Tzu

A disciplined force overwhelms a disordered one effortlessly.

In dating, when your life is full and your standards stable, you don't need to convince anyone of your worth. Your presence does the work.

FINAL IMAGE

Sun Tzu ends with force breaking loose like water released from a dam.

That is what clarity feels like. No chasing. No forcing. No speeches. Just momentum. And by the time action occurs, the outcome is already decided.

CHAPTER 5

ENERGY
Masculine Pursuit Is Not Optional

"The control of a large force is the same principle as the control of a few men: it is merely a question of dividing up their numbers."

- Sun Tzu

Sun Tzu opens with a truth women need tattooed on their frontal lobes: Managing a large force is no different than managing a small one. It's not about size. It's about structure.

Dating chaos doesn't happen because there are too many men, too many options, or too many feelings. It happens because the energy is unmanaged.

IT'S NOT THE NUMBER OF MEN, IT'S THE SIGNALS

Sun Tzu says fighting with a large army is the same as fighting with a small one. The difference is signals and coordination.

Dating translation: It doesn't matter if he's busy, powerful, important, popular, or drowning in options. If his actions are unclear, his interest is unclear.

Men who want you signal it.
Men who don't create noise.

Consistency is a signal. Effort is a signal. Plans are a signal. Confusion is also a signal. Just not the one you want.

DIRECT VS INDIRECT ENERGY

"In all fighting, the direct method may be used for joining battle, but indirect methods will be needed in order to secure victory."

-   Sun Tzu

Sun Tzu introduces direct and indirect maneuvers.

Direct energy is obvious:
- Asking you out
- Making plans
- Following through

Indirect energy is setup:
- Creating anticipation
- Leading the pace
- Removing access to provoke movement

Women get this wrong constantly. They apply direct energy when indirect energy is required. They chase. They clarify. They push. Masculine energy responds to absence, not pressure.

MOMENTUM COMES FROM WEAK POINTS

Sun Tzu says impact happens when strength meets weakness.

Dating truth: Men move when they sense they might lose access not when you explain your feelings. Your availability is not leverage. Your *withholding* is. If he is comfortable, nothing moves. If he is uncertain, he advances.

INDIRECT STRATEGY NEVER RUNS OUT

Sun Tzu calls indirect tactics inexhaustible. Why? Because polarity renews itself.

You pull back. He leans forward. You pause. He pursues. This is not manipulation. This is physics. When women try to generate momentum themselves, attraction collapses.

39

FIVE NOTES. ENDLESS MUSIC.

"There are not more than five musical notes, yet the combinations of these five give rise to more melodies than can ever be heard."

- Sun Tzu

Sun Tzu reminds us that a few basic elements create infinite variation.

Dating doesn't require new tricks. It requires mastery of fundamentals:

- Availability
- Mystery
- Warmth
- Distance
- Timing

Women overcomplicate dating because they don't trust simplicity. Men do.

INFINITE VARIATIONS

"There are not more than five primary colors (blue, yellow, red, white, and black), yet in combination they produce more hues than can ever be seen."

- Sun Tzu

There are only a few basic elements in dating: attraction, timing, communication, boundaries, power. That's it. No secret sixth color. No hidden cheat code. And yet, the combinations are endless.

A pause can mean confidence or indifference. Silence can be mystery or avoidance. Desire can be intoxicating or destabilizing, depending on who holds it. What matters isn't the ingredient. It's the mix.

Most people keep looking for a new color instead of mastering composition. They overcomplicate instead of refining.

When you understand how the basics interact, you stop chasing novelty and start creating chemistry. Master the fundamentals. The variations will take care of themselves. That's where the art is.

FLAVOR IS ABOUT BALANCE

"There are not more than five cardinal tastes (sour, acrid, salt, sweet, bitter), yet combinations of them yield more flavors than can ever be tasted."

- Sun Tzu

Dating isn't missing ingredients, it's missing restraint. Everyone wants sweetness without bitterness. Passion without edge. Security without tension. Excitement without risk. That's not chemistry. That's bland.

The depth comes from contrast. A little sharpness makes desire pop. A hint of bitterness gives sweetness meaning. Salt grounds fantasy. Heat keeps things alive.

When everything is pleasant, nothing is memorable. The most intoxicating connections aren't smooth, they're layered. They surprise you. They linger.

If you want flavor, stop trying to make everything taste "good."

Start letting it taste real. That's what people come back for.

DIRECT + INDIRECT = EVERYTHING

There are only two methods. But their combinations are endless.

Warmth without access.
Interest without pursuit.
Openness without overexposure.

This is how attraction sustains itself.

ENERGY IS CIRCULAR NOT LINEAR

Sun Tzu says direct and indirect flow endlessly into each other.

Dating dies when women make everything linear:
"I like you → I show it → I wait."

Attraction is cyclical: Advance. Pause. Respond. Withdraw.
Men lead when women allow space.

MOMENTUM IS NOT PERSONALITY, IT'S TIMING

"The onset of troops is like the rush of a torrent which will even roll stones along in its course."

- Sun Tzu

Sun Tzu compares attack to a rushing torrent.

Dating truth: When momentum is right, things move fast *without effort.*

If you are forcing progress, the slope is wrong. Stop pushing uphill.

DECISION IS SEXIER THAN EMOTION

"The quality of decision is like the well-timed swoop of a falcon which enables it to strike and destroy its victim."

- Sun Tzu

Sun Tzu praises decisive action.

Men are not confused by women who know what they will tolerate. They are confused by women who say one thing and accept another. Boundaries create clarity. Clarity creates movement.

POWER IS STORED NOT SPENT

Sun Tzu compares energy to a bent crossbow.

Dating translation: Restraint is not passivity. It's stored power.

Women exhaust themselves by firing every arrow immediately. Men respond to potential, not depletion.

CHAOS CAN BE CONTROLLED

Sun Tzu says apparent disorder can exist without real disorder.

Dating truth: You can look relaxed, easygoing, fun while still having iron boundaries. Calm does not mean permissive. Cool does not mean available.

FAKE WEAKNESS REQUIRES REAL STRENGTH

Simulated fear requires courage. Simulated disorder requires discipline.

Translation: Pulling back without spiraling requires emotional regulation. Women who *pretend* not to care while caring deeply lose control. Women who genuinely regulate their attachment win effortlessly.

DECEPTION IS NOT LYING, IT'S PACING

"Thus one who is skillful at keeping the enemy on the move maintains deceitful appearances, according to which the enemy will act. He sacrifices something, that the enemy may snatch at it."

- Sun Tzu

Sun Tzu is explicit: appearances guide action.

Dating translation: You do not reveal everything you feel immediately. Mystery creates pursuit. Oversharing kills it. This is not dishonesty. This is timing.

BAITS ARE NOT BEGGING

"By holding out baits, he keeps him on the march; then with a body of picked men he lies in wait for him."

- Sun Tzu

Sun Tzu says the skilled combatant offers bait.

Dating bait is not chasing. It's warmth. Presence. Then absence. Men chase what moves away not what waits.

COMBINED ENERGY BEATS INDIVIDUAL EFFORT

Sun Tzu emphasizes combined force.

Dating truth: You are not meant to do all the work. If attraction requires constant effort from you, the system is broken. Healthy dynamics move themselves.

ROUND STONES ALWAYS ROLL

Sun Tzu's metaphor is brutal and perfect. Square stones stop. Round stones roll.

Dating translation: Rigid women exhaust men. Flexible, self-contained women create flow. This does not mean tolerating disrespect. It means not clinging.

MOMENTUM DECIDES EVERYTHING

Sun Tzu ends with momentum rolling downhill.

Dating should feel inevitable. If you're asking:
- "Where is this going?"
- "How does he feel?"
- "Why hasn't he…"

The energy is stalled. And stalled energy never leads to victory.

44

FINAL TRUTH

Masculine pursuit is not optional. If you generate the momentum, you carry the relationship. If he generates it, he values it. Energy reveals truth faster than words ever will.

CHAPTER 6

WEAK POINTS AND STRONG
Where Men Fold

Sun Tzu starts with something deceptively simple: Whoever arrives first is rested. Whoever rushes in second is already tired.

Dating translation: The woman who builds a full life and lets men enter it is calm. The woman who rushes toward men is already depleted. Desperation doesn't start loud. It starts tired.

HE WHO CHASES LOSES POSITION

Sun Tzu says the clever combatant imposes his will. He does not absorb the enemy's.

Dating truth: The person who cares more sets the pace unless they stop themselves. If you're rearranging your schedule, overthinking texts, and waiting on his availability, his will is already imposed on you. Power leaks quietly.

ADVANTAGE IS ENTICEMENT. DAMAGE IS CONSEQUENCE

"By holding out advantages to him, he can cause the enemy to approach of his own accord; or, by inflicting damage, he can make it impossible for the enemy to draw near."

- Sun Tzu

Sun Tzu outlines two methods: Entice with advantage, or strike where it hurts.

Dating translation:
- Warmth invites effort
- Withdrawal corrects laziness

You do not yell. You do not explain. You adjust access. Men learn faster from consequence than conversation.

REST IS A LUXURY. MAKE HIM MOVE

Sun Tzu says if the enemy is comfortable, disturb him.

Dating truth: Men coast when women accommodate. If he's comfortable with minimal effort, nothing changes. Removing availability forces recalibration.

SHOW UP WHERE HE IS NOT READY

Sun Tzu says attack where defense is absent.

Dating translation: Stop confronting him directly about commitment. Instead:
- Stop initiating
- Stop accommodating
- Stop explaining

Silence is a flank attack.

MOVE THROUGH EMPTY TERRITORY

Sun Tzu praises movement through undefended land.

Dating truth: A woman who does not chase moves freely. She doesn't argue for attention. She invests where interest already exists.

This is why walking away feels powerful, because it is.

ATTACK ONLY WHAT IS UNGUARDED

Sun Tzu is blunt: only attack undefended points.

Dating translation: Do not try to access emotional depth from emotionally defended men.

If vulnerability is guarded, you don't knock. You leave.

CONFUSION IS A WEAPON

"Hence that general is skillful in attack whose opponent does not know what to defend; and he is skillful in defense whose opponent does not know what to attack."

- Sun Tzu

The best strategists make opponents unsure what to defend or attack.

Dating truth: Predictability kills leverage.

If he knows you'll always answer, wait, forgive, or explain, he relaxes. When patterns change, men pay attention.

INVISIBILITY IS POWER

"O divine art of subtlety and secrecy! Through you we learn to be invisible, through you inaudible; and hence we can hold the enemy's fate in our hands."

- Sun Tzu

Sun Tzu praises invisibility and silence.

Dating translation:
You do not announce exits.
You do not narrate feelings.
You do not crowd intimacy.

Your absence speaks louder than your words ever did.

SPEED PROTECTS YOU

"You may advance and be absolutely irresistible, if you make for the enemy's weak points; you may retire and be safe from pursuit if your movements are more rapid than those of the enemy."

- Sun Tzu

Advance swiftly when attacking weakness. Withdraw faster than pursuit.

Dating truth: When you leave, leave clean. Dragging out endings creates pursuit you don't want and attachment you can't sever.

MAKE HIM ENGAGE OR MAKE HIM REVEAL

Sun Tzu explains how to force engagement indirectly.

Dating translation: You don't ask where this is going. You live as if you're going somewhere regardless. Men reveal intentions when they feel replaced by possibility.

BLUFF IS NOT LYING. IT'S RESTRAINT.

"If we do not wish to fight, we can prevent the enemy from engaging us even though the lines of our encampment be merely traced out on the ground. All we need do is to throw something odd and unaccountable in his way."

- Sun Tzu

Sun Tzu openly endorses bluff.

Dating translation: Calm is not indifference. Silence is not disinterest. Not reacting immediately is emotional intelligence.

UNITY BEATS SCRAMBLING

"By discovering the enemy's dispositions and remaining invisible ourselves, we can keep our forces concentrated, while the enemy's must be divided."

- Sun Tzu

Sun Tzu explains concentration vs division.

Dating truth: A woman aligned with herself is focused. A man unsure of her intentions splits his attention everywhere. Confusion weakens him not you.

UNITY IS LEVERAGE

"We can form a single united body, while the enemy must split up into fractions. Hence there will be a whole pitted against separate parts of a whole, which means that we shall be many to the enemy's few."

- Sun Tzu

Dating power isn't about numbers, it's about cohesion. When you're clear in your standards, boundaries, and self-worth, you move as one body.

You don't contradict yourself. You don't chase and retreat. You don't negotiate against your own needs. Meanwhile, the other side fractures. Mixed signals. Split intentions. One foot in, one foot out. Ego pulling one way, insecurity pulling another.

A unified presence doesn't argue, it *outlasts* confusion. When you are whole, you face fragments. And fragments always lose to clarity. The goal isn't to overpower someone. It's to remain intact while they fall apart. That's leverage.

MAKE HIM OVERDEFEND

"The spot where we intend to fight must not be made known; for then the enemy will have to prepare against a possible attack at several different points; and his forces being thus distributed in many directions, the numbers we shall have to face at any given point will be proportionately few."

- Sun Tzu

Sun Tzu says force the enemy to prepare everywhere.

Dating translation: When your availability becomes uncertain, men hedge. They overthink. They test. They pursue. You stay still.

50

OVERCOMPENSATION CREATES OPENINGS

"For should the enemy strengthen his van, he will weaken his rear; should he strengthen his rear, he will weaken his van; should he strengthen his left, he will weaken his right; should he strengthen his right, he will weaken his left. If he sends reinforcements everywhere, he will everywhere be weak."

- Sun Tzu

When someone tries to cover everything, they protect nothing. If he over-explains, something else goes silent. If he overtexts, his actions thin out. If he locks down one connection, another starts leaking.

Energy is finite. Attention is finite. Every time he reinforces one side, another weakens. People who juggle options reveal themselves through imbalance: presence without consistency, affection without follow-through, availability without depth.

You don't need to confront the chaos. You watch where the effort spikes and where it disappears. The moment someone spreads themselves everywhere, they are strongest in appearance and weakest in truth. Patterns don't lie.

MAKE THEM REACT

"Numerical weakness comes from having to prepare against possible attacks; numerical strength, from compelling our adversary to make these preparations against us."

- Sun Tzu

Power shifts the moment someone starts adjusting themselves *around you*. When you're uncertain, you prepare. When you're chasing, you anticipate. When you're insecure, you overcorrect. That's numerical weakness. Numerical strength comes from the opposite position: being so grounded, so unpredictable, so self-contained that the other person starts rearranging their behavior in response to you.

They hesitate before speaking. They rethink their timing. They wonder what you know. You don't chase information. You don't explain yourself into relevance. You don't prepare for every possible outcome. You become the variable. The person who forces the adjustment controls the dynamic. And the one doing the preparing has already surrendered leverage.

KNOW TIME AND PLACE OR WALK AWAY

"Knowing the place and the time of the coming battle, we may concentrate from the greatest distances in order to fight."

- Sun Tzu

Sun Tzu is ruthless about timing.

Dating truth: If there is no clarity on direction or timing, disengage. Undefined relationships drain energy faster than rejection ever could.

NUMBERS DON'T MATTER IF STRATEGY IS BAD

Sun Tzu says larger forces don't guarantee victory.

Dating translation: More options don't make a man better. Consistency beats abundance every time.

PREVENT HIM FROM FIGHTING AT ALL

"Though the enemy be stronger in numbers, we may prevent him from fighting. Scheme so as to discover his plans and the likelihood of their success."

- Sun Tzu

Sun Tzu explains how to stop engagement entirely.

Dating truth: Indifference ends games faster than confrontation. Men don't chase women who chase back.

STIR HIM TO REVEAL HIMSELF

"Rouse him, and learn the principle of his activity or inactivity. Force him to reveal himself, so as to find out his vulnerable spots."

-   Sun Tzu

Sun Tzu encourages provoking reaction to expose weakness.

Dating translation: Pull back and watch. His response tells you everything.

COMPARE STRENGTHS HONESTLY

"Carefully compare the opposing army with your own, so that you may know where strength is superabundant and where it is deficient."

-   Sun Tzu

Sun Tzu insists on honest assessment.

Dating truth: If you're investing more than he is, the imbalance will cost you. Do not romanticize inequality.

CONCEAL YOUR STRATEGY

"In making tactical dispositions, the highest pitch you can attain is to conceal them; conceal your dispositions, and you will be safe from the prying of the subtlest spies, from the machinations of the wisest brains."

-   Sun Tzu

Sun Tzu says concealment creates safety.

Dating translation: You do not reveal plans, expectations, or timelines prematurely. Privacy preserves power.

LET THEM DEFEAT THEMSELVES

"How victory may be produced for them out of the enemy's own tactics—that is what the multitude cannot comprehend."

-   Sun Tzu

Most people think winning comes from force. It doesn't. It comes from observation. You don't need to outplay someone. You let their own habits expose them. Their patterns. Their impulses. Their tells. The way they push. The way they avoid. The way they repeat the same move and expect a different outcome. The majority can't see this because they're too busy reacting. They think strategy looks loud. Obvious. Aggressive.

Real leverage is quieter. You allow people to reveal their playbook and then step aside while it collapses under its own weight. Victory doesn't always look like attack. Sometimes it looks like patience. And most people never see it coming.

STRATEGY IS INVISIBLE

> *"All men can see the tactics whereby I conquer, but what none can see is the strategy out of which victory is evolved."*
>
> - Sun Tzu

Everyone sees outcomes. No one sees restraint. Dating wins look effortless because they were quiet.

DO NOT REPEAT WHAT WORKED ON SOMEONE ELSE

> *"Do not repeat the tactics which have gained you one victory, but let your methods be regulated by the infinite variety of circumstances."*
>
> - Sun Tzu

Sun Tzu warns against repeating tactics blindly.

Dating truth: Each man reveals himself differently. Stay observant, not formulaic.

WATER ALWAYS SEEKS WEAKNESS

> *"Military tactics are like unto water; for water in its natural course runs away from high places and hastens downwards."*
>
> - Sun Tzu

Sun Tzu's water metaphor is the whole point.

Dating translation: Stop forcing where there is resistance. Flow toward receptivity.

DON'T FIGHT STRENGTH. EXPOSE WEAKNESS

"So in war, the way is to avoid what is strong and to strike at what is weak."

- Sun Tzu

You don't confront someone where they're polished. You don't argue where they're rehearsed. You don't challenge the version they've perfected for display. You move elsewhere.

You watch where they deflect. Where they overreact. Where the confidence drops and the story changes. Strength is usually loud and protected. Weakness hides in the margins.

You don't attack what's reinforced. You apply pressure where the armor thins. That's not cruelty. That's intelligence. Because the quickest way to lose leverage is to fight someone on their strongest ground.

THERE IS NO FIXED FORM

"Water shapes its course according to the nature of the ground over which it flows; the soldier works out his victory in relation to the foe whom he is facing. Therefore, just as water retains no constant shape, so in warfare there are no constant conditions."

- Sun Tzu

Dating has no rules only patterns. Adaptation is intelligence.

HEAVEN-BORN CAPTAINS ADJUST

"He who can modify his tactics in relation to his opponent and thereby succeed in winning, may be called a heaven-born captain."

- Sun Tzu

Women who adjust without panic dominate. Women who cling lose.

EVERYTHING MOVES IN CYCLES

"The five elements (water, fire, wood, metal, earth) are not always equally predominant; the four seasons make way for each other in turn. There are short days and long; the moon has its periods of waning and waxing."

- Sun Tzu

Sun Tzu ends with seasons, waxing and waning.

Dating truth: Attraction has phases. Do not cling to one moment. Those who respect cycles outlast those who demand permanence.

FINAL TRUTH

Men fold at their weak points not when you push, but when you stop holding them up. You were never meant to carry the weight. When you step back, truth steps forward.

CHAPTER 7

MANEUVERING
Texting Is Logistics, Not Love

THE SOVEREIGN LOSES THE WAR WHEN SHE PANICS

"In war, the general receives his commands from the sovereign."

- Sun Tzu

Sun Tzu reminds us that commands come from the sovereign. In dating, *you* are the sovereign.

The moment your nervous system starts issuing orders: *text him again, explain yourself, ask what he meant, secure the situation*, you have been quietly overthrown. Panic masquerades as action. Urgency disguises itself as honesty. But strategy cannot operate from a dysregulated body.

A woman who governs herself calmly forces the battlefield to adjust around her. A woman who reacts forfeits command even if she's technically "right."

ALIGN YOUR RANKS BEFORE YOU ADVANCE

"Having collected an army and concentrated his forces, he must blend and harmonize the different elements thereof before pitching his camp."

- Sun Tzu

Before any army moves, it must be internally unified. Before you date anyone, the same rule applies.

Self-esteem, standards, boundaries, sleep, routines, these are not "self-care extras."

They are your supply chain. If your internal army is in civil war, the first man with charm, attention, or sexual tension will annex your emotional economy without resistance.

This is why unstable seasons produce bad dating decisions. You're not choosing poorly. You're negotiating under siege.

MANEUVERING IS HARD BECAUSE CHAOS FEELS FAMILIAR

"After that, comes tactical maneuvering, than which there is nothing more difficult. The difficulty of tactical maneuvering consists in turning the devious into the direct, and misfortune into gain."

- Sun Tzu

Sun Tzu says maneuvering is the most difficult part of war.

Dating feels hard for the same reason. Not because men are confusing, but because restraint feels foreign to people raised on emotional adrenaline.

Maneuvering means resisting the urge to sprint toward what feels familiar. It means slowing down long enough to see patterns, pacing, intent. Strategy feels boring to the untrained nervous system. But boredom is often peace in disguise.

GHOSTING IS INTEL, NOT A TRAGEDY

"Thus, to take a long and circuitous route, after enticing the enemy out of the way, and though starting after him, to contrive to reach the goal before him, shows knowledge of the artifice of deviation."

- Sun Tzu

When a man disappears, many women treat it as emotional catastrophe. Strategically, it's reconnaissance.

Ghosting reveals:
- conflict avoidance

- low emotional stamina
- poor communication under pressure

None of these are mysteries worth solving. The mistake is trying to *interpret* the behavior instead of *using* the information. A detour is not an invitation to build a personality profile, it's a signal to re-route.

DISCIPLINE DATES LIKE A CEO
DESPERATION DATES LIKE A FLASH SALE

"Maneuvering with an army is advantageous; with an undisciplined multitude, most dangerous.

- Sun Tzu

Sun Tzu warns against disorderly maneuvering. In dating, disorder looks like urgency.

A disciplined woman:
- moves intentionally
- responds instead of reacts
- dates with optionality

An undisciplined woman:
- rushes intimacy
- over-explains
- negotiates against herself

One builds equity. The other issues refunds.

PACE IS POWER

"If you set a fully equipped army in march in order to snatch an advantage, the chances are that you will be too late. On the other hand, to detach a flying column for the purpose involves the sacrifice of its baggage and stores."

- Sun Tzu

Move too fast and you lose supplies. Move too slow and you lose timing. Rush intimacy and you lose leverage. Delay clarity and you lose time.

Correct pacing keeps you powerful, observant, and unexhausted. Incorrect pacing leaves you depleted and negotiating from fear. In dating, the bill always arrives later and it's higher when you rush.

FORCED EMOTIONAL MARCHES DESTROY LEADERS

"Thus, if you order your men to roll up their buff-coats, and make forced marches without halting day or night, covering double the usual distance at a stretch, doing a hundred li in order to wrest an advantage, the leaders of all your three divisions will fall into the hands of the enemy."

- Sun Tzu

Sun Tzu warns against forced marches.

Dating equivalents include:
- texting all day
- over-giving early
- trying to "secure" interest
- doing emotional labor for potential

These behaviors exhaust your best leaders: dignity, mystery, discernment. No army wins when its leaders collapse first.

OVER-INVESTMENT BREAKS FORMATION

"The stronger men will be in front, the jaded ones will fall behind, and on this plan only one-tenth of your army will reach its destination."

- Sun Tzu

When you invest unevenly, you become unstable. Intense. Then tired. Then gone. Then back again. That's not passion. That's a broken supply chain. Consistency is a privilege earned not a resource to be drained upfront.

OVEREXTENSION COSTS YOU YOUR LEADERS

If you march fifty li to outmaneuver the enemy, you will lose the leader of your first division, and only half your force will reach the goal. If you march thirty li, most of your army survives.

Dating translation: Overextension is not enthusiasm. It is attrition. When you push too hard too early: labels, pressure, emotional urgency, you don't just risk rejection. You lose your strongest positions first: composure, clarity, self-respect. Fifty li dating looks like trying to secure outcomes before behavior supports them. Thirty li looks like steady movement, measured investment, and time doing its job. Do not sprint into emotional depth with someone still operating at the level of "wyd."

Arriving early means nothing if you arrive depleted. Victory favors the woman who reaches the moment whole, not the one who arrives fastest.

WITHOUT BAGGAGE, PROVISIONS, AND SUPPLY BASES. YOU LOSE.

> *"We may take it then that an army without its baggage-train is lost; without provisions it is lost; without bases of supply it is lost."*
>
> - Sun Tzu

Dating translation: If you have no friends, no routines, no goals, no life outside him, you are an army without supply lines. And you will start eating crumbs like they're a meal.

NO ALLIANCES UNTIL YOU KNOW NEIGHBORS' DESIGNS.

> *"We cannot enter into alliances until we are acquainted with the designs of our neighbors."*
>
> - Sun Tzu

Don't enter "exclusive" until you know his ecosystem: exes, addictions, chaos, lifestyle, values, character under stress. Chemistry is not reconnaissance.

KNOW THE TERRAIN BEFORE YOU MARCH

"We are not fit to lead an army on the march unless we are familiar with the face of the country—its mountains and forests, its pitfalls and precipices, its marshes and swamps.

- Sun Tzu

Sun Tzu never sends troops blindly. Neither should you.

Late-night hangouts. "Netflix at my place." Vague plans. Situationship language. Some terrain is designed to trap you in ambiguity. Strategy means recognizing where you are before you move.

SCOUT BEFORE YOU ADVANCE

"We shall be unable to turn natural advantages to account unless we make use of local guides."

- Sun Tzu

Local guide = your intuition, your friend who hates him, your past pattern recognition. If everyone who loves you is like "something is off" … that is your scouting report.

CONCEALMENT IS STRATEGY, NOT DECEPTION

"In war, practice dissimulation, and you will succeed."

- Sun Tzu

Yes. This means you don't reveal everything. You don't announce your feelings first. You don't show your whole hand because he smiled at you twice.

MOVE ONLY WHEN THE FIELD FAVORS YOU

"Whether to concentrate or to divide your troops, must be decided by circumstances."

- Sun Tzu

Don't move because you miss him. Move because he made a clear play: plans, effort, consistency. If there's no advantage, you stay still.

CONCENTRATION IS EARNED, NOT ASSUMED

"Let your rapidity be that of the wind, your compactness that of the forest.

- Sun Tzu

Sometimes you focus on one man. Sometimes you keep dating. The decision is based on behavior, not fantasy.

DETACH QUICKLY, STAND UNMOVED

"In raiding and plundering be like fire, in immovability like a mountain."

- Sun Tzu

Fast like wind = quick to detach from disrespect.
Steady like forest = unshaken by hot-and-cold.

CUT CLEAN OR HOLD FIRM

"Let your plans be dark and impenetrable as night, and when you move, fall like a thunderbolt.?

- Sun Tzu

If you're going to cut him off, do it clean. If you're holding your boundary, do not wobble. Mountains do not "just check in."

EXIT WITHOUT WARNING

"When you plunder a countryside, let the spoil be divided amongst your men; when you capture new territory, cut it up into allotments for the benefit of the soldiery."

- Sun Tzu

Do not warn him you're leaving. Do not "prepare him emotionally" for consequences. You move once. Cleanly. That's thunderbolt behavior.

REWARD INVESTMENT, NOT POTENTIAL

"Ponder and deliberate before you make a move.

- Sun Tzu

Dating translation: When he invests, reward appropriately. Warmth. Appreciation. Reciprocity. But don't give him your whole kingdom because he did the bare minimum.

DO NOTHING WHILE COMPROMISED

"He will conquer who has learnt the artifice of deviation. Such is the art of maneuvering."

\- Sun Tzu

If you're emotional, do nothing. If you're triggered, do nothing. If you're horny, especially do nothing.

TEXTING IS LOGISTICS, NOT LOVE

"The Book of Army Management says: On the field of battle, the spoken word does not carry far enough: hence the institution of gongs and drums. Nor can ordinary objects be seen clearly enough: hence the institution of banners and flags."

\- Sun Tzu

Sun Tzu used drums and banners to communicate clearly.

Texting serves the same function. Texting is for:
- Plans
- Confirmations
- timing

It is not for emotional negotiation, reassurance loops, or essays. If you're writing paragraphs, you're already maneuvering from weakness.

MOVE ONLY WHEN THERE IS ADVANTAGE

Do not move because you miss him.
Do not move because you're lonely.
Do not move because silence makes you anxious.

Move when there is advantage:
- consistent effort
- clear plans
- reciprocal investment

If there's no advantage, you stay still. Stillness is not passivity. It is command.

SET STANDARDS OR INVITE CHAOS

"Gongs and drums, banners and flags, are means whereby the ears and eyes of the host may be focused on one particular point."

- Sun Tzu

Your "signals" are standards: consistency required, respect required, effort required. If your signals are unclear, men act like untrained troops.

ALIGN FIRST, THEN ENGAGE

"The host thus forming a single united body, is it impossible either for the brave to advance alone, or for the cowardly to retreat alone. This is the art of handling large masses of men."

- Sun Tzu

When you're aligned, you don't:

- chase impulsively
- retreat from fear
- over-explain for comfort
  You move as one unit.

DON'T DATE IN THE DARK

"In night-fighting, then, make much use of signal-fires and drums, and in fighting by day, of flags and banners, as a means of influencing the ears and eyes of your army."

- Sun Tzu

Night-fighting = ambiguity hours. Late night. Alcohol. Lust. Loneliness.

That's when you need stronger signals: boundaries, delays, clean exits.

Day-fighting = clarity hours. Plans. Real dates. Real consistency.

HOT-AND-COLD IS ATTRITION

"A whole army may be robbed of its spirit; a commander-in-chief may be robbed of his presence of mind."

- Sun Tzu

Hot-and-cold drains your spirit. Mixed signals steal your presence of mind. If you feel "off your game," that's not romance. That's strategic depletion.

NEVER DECIDE WHILE DEPLETED

"Now a soldier's spirit is keenest in the morning; by noonday it has begun to flag; and in the evening, his mind is bent only on returning to camp."

- Sun Tzu

Your standards are strongest when you're rested and fed. By midnight, you're vulnerable and negotiating with your own loneliness. Eat. Sleep. Then decide.

WAIT OUT HIS EGO

"A clever general, therefore, avoids an army when its spirit is keen, but attacks it when it is sluggish and inclined to return. This is the art of studying moods."

- Sun Tzu

Don't argue with a man when he's smug, empowered, or entertained by options. Let time and absence humble him. Then see what returns.

SILENCE EXPOSES EVERYTHING

"Disciplined and calm, to await the appearance of disorder and hubbub amongst the enemy:—this is the art of retaining self-possession."

- Sun Tzu

A calm woman terrifies men who rely on chaos. She doesn't react. She observes. And their disorder shows itself without her lifting a finger.

STAY FED, STAY POWERED

"To be near the goal while the enemy is still far from it, to wait at ease while the enemy is toiling and struggling, to be well-fed while the enemy is famished:—this is the art of husbanding one's strength."

- Sun Tzu

Translation: Have your life together. Your self-worth fed. Your plans set. So, you are not starving for his attention like it's oxygen.

DON'T SABOTAGE STABILITY

"To refrain from intercepting an enemy whose banners are in perfect order, to refrain from attacking an army drawn up in calm and confident array:—this is the art of studying circumstances."

- Sun Tzu

If he is consistent, clear, respectful, don't sabotage it with anxious tests. If the energy is stable, stop poking it.

DON'T CHASE WHAT'S LEAVING

"It is a military axiom not to advance uphill against the enemy, nor to oppose him when he comes downhill."

- Sun Tzu

Don't chase a man who is retreating.
Don't fight a man who's already decided.
You'll just break your own ankles.

DON'T BITE THE BAIT

"Do not pursue an enemy who simulates flight; do not attack soldiers whose temper is keen."

- Sun Tzu

If he pulls away to see if you chase, do not chase. If he's reactive and hostile, do not engage. That's bait.

DENY ACCESS WITHOUT EXPLANATION

"Do not swallow a bait offered by the enemy."

- Sun Tzu

Bait = "I miss you" at 11:47 PM with no plan.
Bait = "I'm not ready" but wants access.
Also: don't chase closure from a man leaving.
Let him go home. Alone.

END IT CLEAN OR DON'T END IT

"When you surround an army, leave an outlet free. Such is the art of warfare."

- Sun Tzu

When you end things, end cleanly.
No humiliation. No cornering.
Leave an outlet so he doesn't rage, spiral, or retaliate.

You don't need to destroy him.
You need to remove him.

CHAPTER 8

VARIATION OF TACTICS
If He's Confusing, Change the System

THE SOVEREIGN GIVES THE COMMAND.
YOU EXECUTE IT.

"In war, the general receives his commands from the sovereign, collects his army and concentrates his forces."

- Sun Tzu

You are not dating to "see what happens."
That's not romance, that's gambling with mascara on.

The command is: protect your peace, pick the worthy, and don't die on the hill of a man who still thinks "communication" is reacting to your Instagram story.

THE TERRAIN RULES
(A.K.A. STOP CAMPING IN DUMB PLACES)

Sun Tzu drops five terrain truths and every single one applies to modern dating—Difficult country: do not encamp.

If it's confusing, inconsistent, vague, emotionally unavailable, or you need a spreadsheet to track his behavior... Do not set up a cute little emotional Airbnb there. That's not "giving it time." That's squatting.

High roads intersect: join allies.

When dating feels murky, consult your allies: friends, therapist, your group chat with the one savage friend who never gets dickmatized. If you isolate, you lose perspective. If you stay connected, you stay sober.

Dangerously isolated positions: do not linger.

If you're the only one trying, initiating, clarifying, and keeping the connection alive… you are in an isolated outpost. Leave. You are not the National Guard.

Hemmed-in situations: use stratagem.

If you feel boxed in by his mixed signals, you don't plead. You pivot.

Stratagem = change access. Change pace. Change the rules. Less availability. More observation. No emotional labor.

Desperate position: fight.

If a man is actively disrespectful, humiliating, gaslighting, or playing games that erode your self-respect, you don't "heal it."

You fight.

Fight = block, delete, vanish, protect your dignity like it's a designer bag and he's holding a glass of red wine.

THE FIVE "DO NOTs"
(YES, INCLUDING "DON'T OBEY")

Sun Tzu says there are:

Roads you must not follow.

Some roads lead straight to hell:
- late-night "come over"
- "I'm not looking for anything serious"
- "I'm just really busy right now"
- "I don't like labels"
- "Let's see where this goes"

That's a scenic route to emotional bankruptcy.

Armies you must not attack.

Sometimes he's not worth confronting. If you can't create real change, you don't waste your energy "holding him accountable" like you're his HR rep. Conserve your troops.

Towns you must not besiege.

Do not besiege a man into commitment. A man who needs to be cornered into loving you will punish you for it later. If it requires pressure, it isn't yours.

Positions you must not contest.

Some battles aren't winnable because the prize is trash. Winning him doesn't make him a prize. It makes you his caretaker.

Commands of the sovereign which must not be obeyed.

This is the most savage one. Sometimes your "sovereign" is not your higher self. It's your trauma. It's your attachment. It's your ego screaming: "Prove you're chosen."

There are commands inside you that should not be obeyed.

- "Text him again."
- "Explain it better."
- "Maybe I'm asking too much."
- "Be chill so he doesn't leave."

No.

THE WOMAN WHO UNDERSTANDS VARIATION WINS

"The general who thoroughly understands the advantages that accompany variation of tactics knows how to handle his troops."

- Sun Tzu

Sun Tzu says the general who understands variation knows how to handle troops.

71

Dating translation: The woman who adapts is undefeated. She doesn't keep using "be patient" on a man who needs consequences. She doesn't use "communication" on a man who needs removal. She doesn't use "support" on a man who needs accountability. She changes tactics based on behavior.

KNOWING THE MAP IS NOT THE SAME AS USING IT

"The general who does not understand these, may be well acquainted with the configuration of the country, yet he will not be able to turn his knowledge to practical account."

- Sun Tzu

You can know every red flag in the world and still ignore them because he's hot and said you're "different."

Topographical knowledge without flexibility equals delusion.

"FIVE ADVANTAGES" ARE NOT ALWAYS ADVANTAGES

"So, the student of war who is unversed in the art of war of varying his plans, even though he be acquainted with the Five Advantages, will fail to make the best use of his men."

- Sun Tzu

Sun Tzu basically says: even if something seems obviously smart, don't do it if it's a trap.

Dating example:
- The short road is "just go over" — trap.
- The isolated army is "he's vulnerable right now" — trap.
- The weak town is "he's having a hard week" — trap.
- The stormable position is "he's single and texting daily" — trap.
- The command is "go get clarity" — trap if he's not capable of giving it.

Sometimes what looks like a win is just a faster loss.

BLEND ADVANTAGE AND DISADVANTAGE

"Hence in the wise leader's plans, considerations of advantage and of disadvantage will be blended together."

- Sun Tzu

Always ask:

- "What's the upside?"
- "What's the hidden cost?"

Because men come with subscription fees: Anxiety, Confusion, Time drain, Self-doubt, Reduced standards. If the cost is high, the advantage better be real.

TEMPERED EXPECTATION CREATES CLEAN VICTORY

"If our expectation of advantage be tempered in this way, we may succeed in accomplishing the essential part of our schemes."

- Sun Tzu

If you temper the fantasy with reality, you win. If you don't, you get blindsided and then act shocked like he didn't show you exactly who he was on Date Two when he said, "I'm just not very emotional."

IN DIFFICULTY, SEIZE ADVANTAGE

"If, on the other hand, in the midst of difficulties we are always ready to seize an advantage, we may extricate ourselves from misfortune."

- Sun Tzu

If you're in a hard moment: confused, disappointed, uncertain, seize the advantage: The advantage is not "talking it out."
The advantage is clarity through action:

- Pull back
- Observe
- Require effort
- Stop feeding the dynamic

Hard moments are where women either level up or relapse.

73

REDUCE HOSTILE CHIEFS: DAMAGE THEM + KEEP THEM BUSY

"Reduce the hostile chiefs by inflicting damage on them; and make trouble for them, and keep them constantly engaged; hold out specious allurements, and make them rush to any given point."

- Sun Tzu

This sounds violent. It's dating. Relax.

Hostile chief = emotionally lazy man who benefits from your softness. How you reduce him:

- Remove comfort
- Remove access
- Remove emotional labor
- Keep him engaged in effort or he gets nothing

Specious allurements = don't argue.

Let him chase the mirage of "losing you."

(If he doesn't chase, congratulations, you just saved six months.)

RELY ON YOUR READINESS, NOT THEIR GOOD INTENTIONS

"The art of war teaches us to rely not on the likelihood of the enemy's not coming, but on our own readiness to receive him; not on the chance of his not attacking, but rather on the fact that we have made our position unassailable."

- Sun Tzu

Never rely on:

- "He probably didn't mean it"
- "He's just stressed"
- "He's scared because he likes me"

Rely on readiness:

- boundaries
- standards
- self-control
- exit ability

You are not protected by his intentions. You are protected by your position.

THE FIVE DANGEROUS FAULTS (Dating Edition)

Sun Tzu lists five faults in a general. Here they are in women dating men:

(1) Recklessness → destruction

This is the woman who says:
"I don't care, I'm going all in."

And then cries in a bathrobe two weeks later holding her phone like it's a hostage negotiation.

(2) Cowardice → capture

This is the woman who won't risk losing him, so she accepts less. That's how you get captured into a situationship prison.

(3) Hasty temper → provoked by insults

He baits you. You explode. Now you look "crazy."
Do not play his game.

Silence is higher status than reacting.

(4) Delicacy of honor → thin-skinned shame spiral

You feel embarrassed that you cared.
So you try to "win" by being colder than you actually are.

That's not strategy. That's ego in a trench coat.

(5) Over-solicitude for your men → worry and trouble

This is the caretaker disease.

You start managing his moods, protecting his feelings, helping him "heal," excusing everything.

Ma'am. You are dating. Not adopting.

CHAPTER 9

THE ARMY ON THE MARCH
Watch actions, not words.

THE TERRAIN RULES
(Where you "camp" matters)

1) Pass quickly over mountains, stay near valleys. Don't linger in barren, dry, high-effort dating situations. Stay near what feeds you: consistency, warmth, clarity, effort. If it's emotionally dehydrating, keep moving.

2) Camp on high places facing the sun. Don't climb heights to fight. Pick situations where you have leverage and visibility: you're respected, you're wanted, you're not guessing. But don't chase "winning" by fighting uphill for someone who won't meet you halfway.

3) After crossing a river, get far away from it. After a boundary, after a breakup, after a "we need to talk," don't hover at the edge. Create distance so you can see the whole map clearly.

4) Don't meet them mid-stream. Let half cross, then strike. If he's "coming back," don't jump in the river to greet him. Let him prove it consistently first. Half across = consistent behavior over time. Then you decide.

5) If you're anxious to fight, don't meet him near the river he must cross. If you want the truth, don't prevent the test. Give him enough room to show what he'll do on his own.

6) Moor higher than the enemy, facing the sun. Don't move upstream to meet him. Stay positioned above the chaos. Don't chase the current. If you're moving "upstream" emotionally to drag a connection forward, you're already losing.

7) Salt-marshes: get over them quickly. If it's low-quality, draining, exposed, and dry… don't unpack your heart there.

8) If forced to fight in a salt-marsh, keep water/grass near, back to trees. If you must have a hard conversation, do it from support and stability: friends, receipts, boundaries, self-control. No emotional free-falling.

9) Flat country: accessible position, rising ground right/rear. Choose dating positions where you can exit easily and keep your dignity behind you. Don't date in a way that traps you.

10) Master the four terrains: mountains, rivers, marshes, plains. Know the four dating terrains too:
- High effort / low return
- Emotional floods
- Muddy uncertainty
- Boring stability (which is actually where good love lives)

11) Prefer high ground to low, sunny to dark. Choose clarity over secrecy. Choose openness over ambiguity. Choose "I like you and I'm showing it" over "guess my intentions."

12) Care for your men, camp on hard ground, avoid disease = victory. If you protect your energy and keep your standards firm, you avoid the disease: confusion, anxiety, obsession, and "why am I acting like this?"

13) Hills/banks: take the sunny side, slope on right rear. Put yourself in the advantageous position: you're calm, you're clear, you're not desperate, you're not negotiating for basic effort.

14) Swollen river with foam: wait until it subsides. If he's in chaos, anger, addiction, a divorce, a midlife spiral, or "I'm not ready"... wait. Do not try to build a relationship in a flood.

15) Avoid cliffs, torrents, hollows, confined places, thickets, quagmires, crevasses. Dating version: avoid situations that trap you, hide truth, and limit movement:

- secret relationships
- "we can't be seen"
- "I'm still living with my ex"
- "I don't do labels"
- "I'm just private" (but somehow public everywhere else)

16) Keep away from those places; make the enemy approach them. Don't go into his messy terrain. Make him come to yours: clarity, consistency, standards.

17) Search nearby cover: hills, ponds, reeds, thick woods = ambush/spies. Watch for hidden threats:

- the "female best friend"
- the ex "who's crazy"
- the roommate "who's basically family"
- the phone he guards like nuclear codes

Search the perimeter early. Don't be shocked later.

THE SIGN-READING RULES
(Behavior tells the truth)

18) If he's close and quiet, he trusts his position. If he's staying near but not progressing, he thinks he has you locked.

19) If he stays aloof and provokes, he wants you to advance. That's baiting. He wants effort from you so he can keep power without committing.

20) If his camp is easy to access, it's a bait. If he gives you just enough attention to keep you hooked, that's not kindness. That's strategy.

21) Movement in trees = advancing. Screens in grass = trying to make you suspicious. If he suddenly gets "busy," changes patterns, scrambles logistics, or becomes vague, something shifted. Sometimes it's a real move. Sometimes it's a fake-out to make you chase.

22) Birds flying up = ambush. Startled beasts = sudden attack. If the vibe changes fast, people act weird, mutuals get quiet, or his behavior jolts—something's under it. Your nervous system notices before your logic does.

23) Dust signals: high column = chariots; low wide = infantry; branching = parties collecting wood; little clouds = encamping. Translation: read the TYPE of movement.

- Big obvious gestures (grand dates, big talk) can be performance.
- Quiet consistent steps (planning, follow-through) are real.
- Scattered behavior (random texts, inconsistent meetups) means he's juggling.
- Small logistical movements (routine effort) means he's settling in.

24) Humble words + more prep = about to advance. Violent language + acting aggressive = retreat. When a man gets suddenly "sweet" while quietly positioning himself, he's moving. When he's loud, dramatic, threatening, or mean, it's often because he's losing control and backing out.

25) Light chariots on the wings = forming for battle. If he starts managing optics: who sees you, where you go, what you post. he's preparing for conflict or concealment.

26) Peace proposals without real commitment = plot. "I want to fix things" with no changed behavior is not peace. It's a stall tactic.

27) Lots of running + falling into rank = critical moment. When he suddenly tightens up behavior: responds fast, plans dates, clarifies, something forced a decision. Maybe you pulled back. Maybe another woman appeared. Maybe he sensed loss.

28) Some advance, some retreat = lure. Hot/cold is not "conflicted." It's a technique.

29) Leaning on spears = hungry. If he's low-energy, low-effort, "I'm tired," "life is hard," but still wants girlfriend benefits? He's operating from depletion and taking from you.

30) Water carriers drinking first = thirst. Watch who takes care of themselves before they serve the relationship. If he's grabbing benefits first: sex, attention, emotional labor before offering stability, he's thirsty, not serious.

31) Sees advantage but doesn't take it = exhausted. If he "likes you" but won't claim you, show up, plan, or deepen… he either can't or won't. Either way, don't volunteer to be the charger.

32) Birds gather = unoccupied. Night clamour = nervousness. If his life looks empty where a girlfriend should fit, that's a sign. If he's anxious at night, spiraling, blowing up your phone late, that's instability talking.

33) Camp disturbance = weak authority. Flags shifting = sedition. Angry officers = weary men. Translation:
- chaos in his life = he can't lead a relationship
- shifting stories = deception
- irritability = burnout, resentment, or guilt

34) Feeding horses grain, killing cattle, no cooking pots = fight to the death. If he starts making drastic moves: big speeches, big promises, big panic behavior, he may be in "last stand" mode. That's not always love. Sometimes that's fear of losing control.

35) Whispering in knots = disaffection. If his friends act weird, he hides messages, people "don't know about you," or there's quiet side chatter, there's internal dissent. Usually: other women, unfinished business, or a double life.

36) Too many rewards = resources low. Too many punishments = distress. If he starts love-bombing, gifting, flattering nonstop, suddenly "best boyfriend ever" out of nowhere—he may be buying time. If he's harsh, critical, punishing, cold, he's in distress or trying to dominate.

37) Starts with bluster, then fears numbers = low intelligence. A man who talks big then collapses under real relationship responsibility is not a leader. He's marketing.

38) Compliments via envoys = wants a truce. If he sends friends, indirect messages, or soft "checking in" texts, he wants calm without accountability.

39) Marches up angry and just stands there = be vigilant. If he's looming: watching your stories, staying nearby, keeping access, but not committing or leaving… That's a setup. Stay sharp.

40) If numbers are equal, don't do frontal attack; concentrate, watch, get reinforcements. If you don't have leverage, don't go head-on with emotion. Pull your energy together, observe behavior, and strengthen your support system.

41) No forethought, makes light of opponent = gets captured. If you underestimate how selfish, strategic, or avoidant someone can be, you'll get played. Never date assuming someone is "nice" because they smiled.

42) Punish before attachment = useless. No punishment after attachment = useless. Early dating: don't go harsh, don't go controlling. But once a pattern is clear and you're invested, boundaries must exist or the relationship rots.

43) Humanity first, then iron discipline. Warm heart, hard standards. Soft love, firm boundaries. Kindness without consequences is how women end up raising grown men.

44) Enforced commands in training = disciplined army. If you say what you require and you consistently enforce it, your dating life becomes peaceful. If you cave every time, you train people to ignore you.

45) Confidence + insist orders are obeyed = mutual gain. The best relationships are: "I trust you" + "I still require respect." That's where both people win.

CHAPTER 10

TERRAIN

Dating apps are hostile territory.

THE 6 TYPES OF TERRAIN
(aka the 6 app ecosystems)

"We may distinguish six kinds of terrain, to wit: Accessible ground; entangling ground; temporizing ground; narrow passes; precipitous heights; positions at a great distance from the enemy."

- Sun Tzu

1) Accessible ground.

This is easy dating: clear interest, easy scheduling, consistent effort.

Translation: it shouldn't feel like you're storming Normandy just to get a phone call.

2) Entangling ground

This is the situationship swamp. Easy to enter, hard to exit with your dignity intact.

Translation: "Let's just see where it goes" is quicksand with a cute font.

3) Temporizing ground

The stalled zone. Nothing moves, nothing ends, nothing becomes real.

Translation: he's "not sure," but also somehow sure enough for sex.

4) Narrow passes

High stakes bottlenecks: you get one lane, one chance, one mistake and you're dead.

Translation: meeting his friends, defining the relationship, exclusivity talk, "what are we?"

5) Precipitous heights

Power imbalance territory. One person holds the advantage.

Translation: celebrity energy, rich-guy status, "I'm too busy," or anyone who makes you feel lucky they replied.

6) Great distance from the enemy

Long distance, emotional distance, avoidant distance.

Translation: you're trying to build intimacy with someone who won't even build a sentence.

HOW TO MOVE THROUGH EACH TERRAIN
Accessible Ground — Mutual Ease

> *"Ground which can be freely traversed by both sides is called accessible."*
>
> -   Sun Tzu

If it's easy for both people, don't sabotage it. Accessible ground in dating is mutual effort, mutual curiosity, and mutual availability. No one is hiding, chasing, or performing. You can reach each other without strategy or strain.

The mistake women make here is mistaking calm for boredom. They introduce drama, distance, or tests to manufacture chemistry, not realizing they're poisoning the very ground that allows something real to grow.

Ease is not a red flag. Peace is not a lack of passion. Consistency is not a trap. If both of you can move freely toward each other, let it be simple. War is not required on safe ground.

Don't lead with access.

"With regard to ground of this nature, be before the enemy in occupying the raised and sunny spots, and carefully guard your line of supplies."

-   Sun Tzu

Be first to secure what matters: clarity, boundaries, self-respect. Guard your supplies = protect your energy, time, body, and attention. Your attention is currency. Stop handing it out like free samples at Costco.

Leaving is easy. Going back costs you

"Ground which can be abandoned but is hard to re-occupy is called entangling.

-   Sun Tzu

Once you exit a toxic dynamic, don't "just check in." That's how you get re-captured emotionally like a dumb little soldier.

Exit only when it counts

"From a position of this sort, if the enemy is unprepared, you may sally forth and defeat him. But if the enemy is prepared for your coming, and you fail to defeat him, then, return being impossible, disaster will ensue."

-   Sun Tzu

If he's not expecting you to leave, leaving works. If he's ready for your patterns and you keep trying the same speech? He'll win.

The stalemate favors the detached

"When the position is such that neither side will gain by making the first move, it is called temporizing ground."

-   Sun Tzu

This is the stalemate where both people are waiting for the other to care more. Spoiler: the person who cares less has the advantage.

Don't bite crumbs

"In a position of this sort, even though the enemy should offer us an attractive bait, it will be advisable not to stir forth, but rather to retreat, thus enticing the enemy in his turn; then, when part of his army has come out, we may deliver our attack with advantage."

- Sun Tzu

Bait = "I miss you," "we should hang," "u up," "I've been thinking."

Don't lunge. Pull back. Make him come into clarity territory. Then you decide.

Set the standard and hold it

"With regard to narrow passes, if you can occupy them first, let them be strongly garrisoned and await the advent of the enemy."

- Sun Tzu

If you set the standard first (exclusivity, respect, timeline), hold it. Don't build a boundary and then abandon it because he smiled.

Don't siege a man's comfort zone

"Should the enemy forestall you in occupying a pass, do not go after him if the pass is fully garrisoned, but only if it is weakly garrisoned."

- Sun Tzu

If he's already locked into "no labels," "casual," "I'm not ready," and he's fortified in that? Don't siege it. But if it's weak (he's wobbly, inconsistent, testing), you can take control with a clean boundary.

Let them rise to you

"With regard to precipitous heights, if you are beforehand with your adversary, you should occupy the raised and sunny spots, and there wait for him to come up."

- Sun Tzu

If you have the upper hand: options, confidence, standards, don't rush downhill for someone unproven. Let them climb.

Stop chasing altitude

"If the enemy has occupied them before you, do not follow him, but retreat and try to entice him away."

- Sun Tzu

If he's acting like the prize while giving you crumbs, stop chasing altitude. Pull back. Let him come down into effort.

Exhaustion is not romance.

"If you are situated at a great distance from the enemy, and the strength of the two armies is equal, it is not easy to provoke a battle, and fighting will be to your disadvantage."

- Sun Tzu

If it takes constant effort to get basic intimacy, you're marching too far. You arrive exhausted, and he's fresh because he didn't do shit.

Dating apps are not neutral ground.

"These six are the principles connected with Earth. The general who has attained a responsible post must be careful to study them."

- Sun Tzu

Dating apps are not romance. They're terrain. You're not "vibing." You're navigating hostile infrastructure.

THE 6 CALAMITIES
(Ways women get taken out)
The six disasters are self-inflicted.

"Now an army is exposed to six several calamities, not arising from natural causes, but from faults for which the general is responsible. These are: Flight; insubordination; collapse; ruin; disorganization; rout."

- Sun Tzu

Translation: it's not "men." It's your strategy.

87

1) Over-investment leads to flight

"Other conditions being equal, if one force is hurled against another ten times its size, the result will be the flight of the former."

- Sun Tzu

If you're emotionally investing ten times more than he is, your system will eventually revolt.

You won't "win him over."
You will flee, burn out, or collapse trying.

This is why chasing feels humiliating instead of romantic. Your nervous system knows you're fighting a war you can't sustain. Stop dating men who require a full-time emotional payroll while offering part-time effort and zero benefits.

2) Imbalance creates insubordination or collapse

"When the common soldiers are too strong and their officers too weak, the result is insubordination. When the officers are too strong and the common soldiers too weak, the result is collapse."

- Sun Tzu

If you're overly available and he's weak, he'll disrespect you. If he's overly demanding and you're depleted, you'll break. Too much effort on one side always corrupts the structure. Either he stops taking you seriously, or you stop functioning properly. Balance isn't fairness, it's survival.

3) Triggered leadership leads to ruin

"When the higher officers are angry and insubordinate, and on meeting the enemy give battle on their own account from a feeling of resentment, before the commander-in-chief can tell whether or no he is in a position to fight, the result is ruin."

- Sun Tzu

Ruin happens when you move while emotionally hijacked. This is where double texting, spiraling, accusations, "closure conversations," and revenge posting live. You fight early, loudly, and without leverage. Not because it's strategic, because you're resentful and raw. Most dating disasters aren't caused by bad men. They're caused by fighting while triggered.

4) Weak command creates chaos

"When the general is weak... orders unclear... no fixed duties... the result is utter disorganization."

- Sun Tzu

If your standards are vague, your boundaries inconsistent, and your rewards disconnected from behavior, your dating life becomes chaos. Men don't know what matters. You don't know what to enforce. Everyone improvises. Confusion spreads. Resentment builds. Clarity is command. Confusion is mutiny.

5) Sending your heart first gets you routed

"When a general, unable to estimate the enemy's strength, allows an inferior force to engage a larger one, or hurls a weak detachment against a powerful one, and neglects to place picked soldiers in the front rank, the result must be a rout."

- Sun Tzu

Dating version: you underestimate his selfishness, send your heart first, and don't protect your front line. Your front line is your time, your body, your emotional access, and your attachment. If those go out unguarded, the rest of you gets wiped. This isn't bad luck. It's poor deployment.

These are six ways of courting defeat. Note them.

"These are six ways of courting defeat, which must be carefully noted by the general who has attained a responsible post."

- Sun Tzu

None of these are accidents. You don't *fall* into them. You walk into them in heels, holding a latte, telling yourself you're being "open," "understanding," or "giving him grace."

Each defeat starts with a choice you rationalize: ignoring imbalance, moving while triggered, sending your heart first, mistaking chaos for chemistry, or staying because you've already invested.

Sun Tzu isn't warning you about bad men. He's warning you about bad command. Leadership in dating means recognizing the moment defeat becomes optional and choosing not to step forward anyway.

GREAT GENERAL ENERGY
(How you actually win)

Hope is not a strategy

"The natural formation of the country is the soldier's best ally; but a power of estimating the adversary, of controlling the forces of victory, and of shrewdly calculating difficulties, dangers and distances, constitutes the test of a great general."

- Sun Tzu

Your best ally is not hope. It's assessment. How far is he? Emotionally. Logistically. Intentionally. Don't pretend distance isn't real.

Knowledge ignored is self-sabotage

"He who knows these things, and in fighting puts his knowledge into practice, will win his battles. He who knows them not, nor practices them, will surely be defeated."

- Sun Tzu

If you keep dating the same pattern in a different body, you're not unlucky. You're undisciplined.

Stop fighting unwinnable men

"If fighting is sure to result in victory, then you must fight, even though the ruler forbid it; if fighting will not result in victory, then you must not fight even at the ruler's bidding."

- Sun Tzu

Stop letting friends hype you into chaos. Stop letting your loneliness draft you into war. Only fight battles you can actually win.

Ego exits are not losses

"The general who advances without coveting fame and retreats without fearing disgrace, whose only thought is to protect his country and do good service for his sovereign, is the jewel of the kingdom."

- Sun Tzu

Don't stay because you want to "prove" you're lovable. Don't chase closure. Don't chase being chosen. Retreating from trash is not embarrassing. It's elite.

Protect the heart you expect to deploy

"Regard your soldiers as your children, and they will follow you into the deepest valleys; look on them as your own beloved sons, and they will stand by you even unto death."

- Sun Tzu

In dating: treat your heart like something you protect and nurture. You don't throw it into gunfire and call it "being open."

Soft leadership creates hard consequences

"If, however, you are indulgent, but unable to make your authority felt; kind-hearted, but unable to enforce your commands; and incapable, moreover, of quelling disorder: then your soldiers must be likened to spoilt children; they are useless for any practical purpose."

- Sun Tzu

Soft standards produce hard consequences. If you keep forgiving what keeps hurting you, you're not kind, you're ungoverned.

Readiness without access is wasted power

"If we know that our own men are in a condition to attack, but are unaware that the enemy is not open to attack, we have gone only halfway towards victory."

- Sun Tzu

You can be ready all day. If he's not receptive, you're shadowboxing.

Open doors mean nothing if you're unstable

"If we know that the enemy is open to attack, but are unaware that our own men are not in a condition to attack, we have gone only halfway towards victory."

- Sun Tzu

If you're depleted, insecure, or unhealed, you'll fumble a good man and call it "bad timing."

Chemistry doesn't cancel bad terrain

"If we know that the enemy is open to attack, and also know that our men are in a condition to attack, but are unaware that the nature of the ground makes fighting impracticable, we have still gone only halfway towards victory."

- Sun Tzu

Sometimes the man is good and you are ready… but the terrain is poison: distance, addiction, ex-wife drama, secret life, incompatible goals. Love doesn't override terrain.

Standards eliminate confusion

"Hence the experienced soldier, once in motion, is never bewildered; once he has broken camp, he is never at a loss."

-   Sun Tzu

When you have standards, you don't get confused by mixed signals. Mixed signals become a signal.

Pattern awareness is dominance

"Hence the saying: If you know the enemy and know yourself, your victory will not stand in doubt; if you know Heaven and know Earth, you may make your victory complete."

-   Sun Tzu

Know him (patterns). Know you (triggers). Know the terrain (apps, culture, incentives). That's how you stop "dating" and start winning.

CHAPTER 11

THE NINE SITUATIONS(HIPS)

"The art of war recognizes nine varieties of ground."
Translation: there are nine dating landscapes, and if you treat them all the same, you die the same.

THE 9 SITUATIONSHIPS

Dating has categories. If you don't name the category, you'll call chaos "connection."

1) Dispersive ground = he's on home turf.

"When a chieftain is fighting in his own territory, it is dispersive ground."

- Sun Tzu

He's comfortable. He has options. He has routine.
Result: he's least motivated to commit because nothing is at stake.

2) Facile ground = he's dipped into your world, but not deeply.

"When he has penetrated into hostile territory, but to no great distance, it is facile ground."

- Sun Tzu

He's participating just enough to keep access.
Result: easy retreat, low investment, high audacity.

3) Contentious ground = whoever controls it gains huge advantage.

"Ground the possession of which imports great advantage to either side, is contentious ground."

- Sun Tzu

This is exclusivity, status, access, commitment, meeting family, defining terms. It's the power point. Everyone fights here.

4) Open ground = both can move freely.

"Ground on which each side has liberty of movement is open ground."
- Sun Tzu

This is early dating done right: clarity is possible, exit is possible. Result: don't try to force-control.

5) Intersecting highways = the key position with multiple alliances.

"Ground which forms the key to three contiguous states, so that he who occupies it first has most of the Empire at his command, is ground of intersecting highways."
- Sun Tzu

This is mutual friends / social circles / industry / city scene / online visibility. Whoever occupies it controls perception and options.

6) Serious ground = you're deep in and cities are behind you.

"When an army has penetrated into the heart of a hostile country, leaving a number of fortified cities in its rear, it is serious ground."
- Sun Tzu

This is when you're attached, sleeping together, bonded, integrated. Retreat now costs you. That's why it's serious.

7) Difficult ground = hard to traverse terrain.

"Mountain forests, rugged steeps, marshes and fens—all country that is hard to traverse: this is difficult ground."
- Sun Tzu

Long distance, trauma history, addiction, chaos schedule, kids + ex war, emotional unavailability. It can be real love, but it's a hard map.

8) Hemmed-in ground = narrow exit routes.

"Ground which is reached through narrow gorges, and from which we can only retire by tortuous paths, so that a small number of the enemy would suffice to crush a large body of our men: this is hemmed in ground."
- Sun Tzu

You can technically leave, but it's complicated: lease, workplace, shared friend group, financial entanglement, kids, public relationship. A small force (one lie) can crush you.

9) Desperate ground = you can only survive by fighting now.

"Ground on which we can only be saved from destruction by fighting without delay, is desperate ground."

- Sun Tzu

This is the moment you finally stop negotiating with the burning house. If you delay, you lose yourself.

WHAT TO DO ON EACH

Don't fight comfort, don't linger in access, don't beg for position.

"On dispersive ground, therefore, fight not. On facile ground, halt not. On contentious ground, attack not."

- Sun Tzu

Dispersive: don't chase comfort men into commitment.

Facile: don't get "stuck" in early access.

Contentious: don't frontal-attack exclusivity with begging. Outmaneuver.

Observe openly, ally strategically.

"On open ground, do not try to block the enemy's way. On ground of intersecting highways, join hands with your allies."

- Sun Tzu

Open: don't control; observe.

Intersecting: use allies: friends, standards, community, reality checks.

Protect your reserves or keep moving.

"On serious ground, gather in plunder. In difficult ground, keep steadily on the march."

- Sun Tzu

Serious: protect your energy, self-worth, and support system.

Difficult: don't camp there hoping it becomes easier. Keep progressing or leave.

Plan your exits quietly and when it's over, end it

"On hemmed-in ground, resort to stratagem. On desperate ground, fight."

- Sun Tzu

Hemmed-in: plan exits quietly and cleanly.

Desperate: stop talking. act.

HOW ELITE PLAYERS WIN

Cut his front from his rear.

"Those who were called skillful leaders of old knew how to drive a wedge between the enemy's front and rear; to prevent co-operation between his large and small divisions; to hinder the good troops from rescuing the bad, the officers from rallying their men."

- Sun Tzu

Cut the connection between his words and his behavior. Also: prevent his "team" (ex, friends, ego, options) from reinforcing his bullshit.

Don't stabilize chaos for him.

"When the enemy's men were scattered, they prevented them from concentrating; even when their forces were united, they managed to keep them in disorder."

- Sun Tzu

If he's inconsistent, don't help him stabilize you into accepting less. If he's suddenly "all in," make him prove it with structure.

Move only when it pays you.

"When it was to their advantage, they made a forward move; when otherwise, they stopped still."

- Sun Tzu

Movement is not virtue. Action is not bravery. And "feeling something" is not leverage.

You do not move from your standards for vibes, loneliness, chemistry, potential, or hope that *this time* will be different. You move when there is payment: clarity, effort, consistency, protection, investment.

If a move costs you dignity, peace, time, or self-respect, it is not a strategy, it is a withdrawal. Stillness is power. Waiting is not weakness. And the woman who can stop herself from advancing without advantage never has to recover from humiliation later.

Access is the real leverage.

"If asked how to cope with a great host of the enemy in orderly array and on the point of marching to the attack, I should say: Begin by seizing something which your opponent holds dear; then he will be amenable to your will."

\- Sun Tzu

In dating: what men hold dear is access. Your access is leverage. If he values you, he'll become responsive.

SPEED + UNGUARDED SPOTS
Leave before he thinks you will.

"Rapidity is the essence of war: take advantage of the enemy's unreadiness, make your way by unexpected routes, and attack unguarded spots."

\- Sun Tzu

Don't telegraph exits for six weeks. Don't debate boundaries for six months. Move clean. Move fast. Hit the unguarded spot: his assumption you'll stay.

INVASION RULES = "YOU WENT DEEP" RULES
Attachment requires discipline.

"The following are the principles to be observed by an invading force: The further you penetrate into a country, the greater will be the solidarity of your troops, and thus the defenders will not prevail against you."

\- Sun Tzu

The more attached you are, the more disciplined you must be. Serious feelings require serious standards.

Keep your life fertile.

"Make forays in fertile country in order to supply your army with food."

- Sun Tzu

Keep your own life fertile: friends, work, creativity, gym, money. Don't live off "his texts."

Don't burn out for love.

"Carefully study the well-being of your men, and do not overtax them. Concentrate your energy and hoard your strength. Keep your army continually on the move, and devise unfathomable plans."

- Sun Tzu

Translation: don't burn out performing for love. Stay moving in your own life. Don't narrate your every thought.

THE "NO ESCAPE" PRINCIPLE

Remove the exit ramp.

"Throw your soldiers into positions whence there is no escape, and they will prefer death to flight. If they will face death, there is nothing they may not achieve. Officers and men alike will put forth their uttermost strength."

- Sun Tzu

Hope is the most dangerous exit ramp in dating. Hope that he will change. Hope that time will clarify. Hope that if you explain it better, he will suddenly rise to the occasion.

As long as that ramp exists, you never fully commit to leaving, and you never fully commit to yourself.

Real change happens when the exits close. When you stop checking. When you stop soft-leaving. When you stop keeping emotional luggage packed "just in case."

When retreat is no longer available, your nervous system stops bargaining and starts obeying. You stop negotiating with crumbs. You stop accepting half-effort as potential. You stop mistaking survival for connection.

Removing the exit ramp is not dramatic. It is decisive. And once you do it, you discover how strong you actually are.

Acceptance kills panic.

"Soldiers when in desperate straits lose the sense of fear. If there is no place of refuge, they will stand firm. If they are in the heart of a hostile country, they will show a stubborn front. If there is no help for it, they will fight hard."

-      Sun Tzu

Panic only exists when you think there is something to save. When you accept "I can lose him," your nervous system stands down. No scrambling. No spiraling. No performance.

Acceptance collapses the illusion that he is your lifeline. The moment you accept loss as survivable, you stop negotiating with fear. You stop chasing reassurance. You stop mistaking anxiety for intuition.

Clarity arrives when escape fantasies disappear. You see patterns instead of potential. Behavior instead of hope. Truth instead of chemistry. Acceptance doesn't make you cold. It makes you dangerous in the best way.

Consistency replaces control.

"Thus, without waiting to be marshalled, the soldiers will be constantly on the qui vive; without waiting to be asked, they will do your will; without restrictions, they will be faithful; without giving orders, they can be trusted."

-      Sun Tzu

When your standards are consistent, you don't have to micromanage. The right man moves toward clarity.

Behavior is the omen.

"Prohibit the taking of omens, and do away with superstitious doubts. Then, until death itself comes, no calamity need be feared."

-      Sun Tzu

Stop reading signs that aren't behavior.
No tarot about "will he text."
The text is the text.

99

Forced effort is not character.

"If our soldiers are not overburdened with money, it is not because they have a distaste for riches; if their lives are not unduly long, it is not because they are disinclined to longevity."

- Sun Tzu

If someone suddenly "changes," it's because the terrain forced it. Don't confuse forced effort with character.

Grief comes before resistance.

"On the day they are ordered out to battle, your soldiers may weep, those sitting up bedewing their garments, and those lying down letting the tears run down their cheeks. But let them once be brought to bay, and they will display the courage of a Chu or a Kuei."

- Sun Tzu

People grieve what they're about to lose. Let them feel it. Don't rescue them from consequence.

THE SNAKE PRINCIPLE = UNIT COHESION
Respond as one system.

"The skillful tactician may be likened to the shuai-jan. Now the shuai-jan is a snake that is found in the Ch'ang mountains. Strike at its head, and you will be attacked by its tail; strike at its tail, and you will be attacked by its head; strike at its middle, and you will be attacked by head and tail both."

- Sun Tzu

Your life must respond like that. If he attacks your self-esteem, your boundaries respond. If he attacks your boundaries, your self-respect responds. No isolated defenses.

Unity beats emotional scatter.

"Asked if an army can be made to imitate the shuai-jan, I should answer, Yes. For the men of Wu and the men of Yüeh are enemies; yet if they are crossing a river in the same boat and are caught by a storm, they will come to each other's assistance just as the left hand helps the right."

- Sun Tzu

Power comes from cohesion, not perfection. A woman who is internally divided leaks energy. One part wants closeness. Another wants safety. Another wants validation. Another wants to disappear. Men feel that fracture immediately.

A unified woman moves as one system. Her standards, boundaries, self-respect, and desire respond together. No part of her undermines another for temporary relief.

Unity is what makes you steady in a storm. It's why mixed signals don't scramble you. It's why pressure doesn't rush you. When your inner ranks are aligned, you stop reacting. You respond.

Storms reveal alignment.

"Hence it is not enough to put one's trust in the tethering of horses, and the burying of chariot wheels in the ground."

- Sun Tzu

Rules don't reveal character. Pressure does. Anyone can behave during easy dates, good moods, and low stakes. Storms strip away performance.

Conflict. Distance. Stress. Uncertainty. That's when alignment shows. Who stabilizes. Who disappears. Who turns cruel. Who turns cooperative.

A storm reveals whether someone is anchored by integrity or held together by convenience. Pay attention to who steadies the boat and who jumps ship the moment the water rises.

Purpose beats self-control.

"The principle on which to manage an army is to set up one standard of courage which all must reach."

- Sun Tzu

Self-control is fragile. It breaks when you're tired, lonely, horny, or hopeful. Purpose holds when willpower collapses. You can delete apps, mute numbers, swear "this time I'm done," and still fold the moment emotion spikes. That's not a discipline problem. That's a purpose problem.

When your standard is clear: what you will and will not tolerate, every part of you moves in the same direction. You stop negotiating with yourself. Unity of purpose does what restraint never can: It makes the wrong move feel impossible, not tempting.

101

One standard, no exceptions.

"How to make the best of both strong and weak—that is a question involving the proper use of ground."

> \- Sun Tzu

Your minimum standard exists to protect you when desire clouds judgment. If it shifts based on attraction, attention, or scarcity, it isn't a standard. It's a mood. Hot men don't get different rules. Charisma doesn't earn exemptions. The moment you start adjusting your baseline to keep access, you teach your nervous system that chemistry outranks self-respect. One standard keeps your footing steady no matter who's in front of you.

THE GENERAL'S ENERGY
Simplify every decision.

"Thus the skillful general conducts his army just as though he were leading a single man, willy-nilly, by the hand."

> \- Sun Tzu

When your strategy is sound, decisions don't require debate. You don't need spreadsheets, group chats, or emotional autopsies. You reduce every choice to one question: does this move protect my dignity, energy, and future, or does it erode them. Complexity is usually avoidance in disguise. Simplicity is command. If a move degrades you, it's a no, even if it feels exciting, romantic, or familiar.

Secrecy keeps order.

"It is the business of a general to be quiet and thus ensure secrecy; upright and just, and thus maintain order."

> \- Sun Tzu

Not everyone deserves access to your inner command room. Broadcasting your plans invites interference, opinions, and emotional sabotage, often from people who benefit from your confusion. Quiet authority creates stability. When you stop explaining yourself, you stop negotiating with noise. Move cleanly, decide privately, and let results speak.

Stop narrating your strategy.
"He must be able to mystify his officers and men by false reports and appearances, and thus keep them in total ignorance."

- Sun Tzu

Dating translation: stop over-explaining your moves. Some people sabotage you with "advice."

Break predictable patterns.
"By altering his arrangements and changing his plans, he keeps the enemy without definite knowledge. By shifting his camp and taking circuitous routes, he prevents the enemy from anticipating his purpose.

- Sun Tzu

Patterns are how you get outplayed. If you always forgive, always return, always explain, always soften, people learn exactly how long they can misbehave before you reset the board for them. Change the rhythm. Interrupt the script. The moment you stop being predictable is the moment dynamics shift. Strategy isn't cruelty, it's refusing to keep reenacting the same loss and calling it hope.

Remove the fallback.
"At the critical moment, the leader of an army acts like one who has climbed up a height and then kicks away the ladder behind him. He carries his men deep into hostile territory before he shows his hand."

- Sun Tzu

Once you decide, remove the fallback option. No "just checking." No "maybe later." No "we can still be friends."

Cut comfort behaviors.
"He burns his boats and breaks his cooking-pots; like a shepherd driving a flock of sheep, he drives his men this way and that, and none knows whither he is going."

- Sun Tzu

Comfort is the enemy of movement. When you keep soothing yourself with familiar habits: stalking his socials, rereading old texts, replaying conversations, scheduling "closure talks" that go nowhere, you're not healing, you're maintaining the attachment. Burning the boats means removing the behaviors that let you retreat emotionally while pretending you're still progressing. No checking. No circling back. No self-administered hope hits. When comfort exits, momentum enters. Discomfort is not danger, it's the signal that you've finally left the old terrain.

Knowing without acting is betrayal.

"To muster his host and bring it into danger:—this may be termed the business of the general."

- Sun Tzu

Seeing the truth changes your responsibility. Once you recognize a pattern, a mismatch, or a slow erosion of respect, neutrality is no longer neutral. Waiting, hoping, or "just observing a little longer" isn't patience, it's avoidance dressed as maturity. Action doesn't always mean confrontation. Sometimes it means withdrawal, boundary enforcement, or silent realignment. But once you know, you must move. Staying still after clarity is how people abandon themselves while calling it love.

ADAPTATION + HUMAN NATURE
Incentives shape behavior.

"The different measures suited to the nine varieties of ground; the expediency of aggressive or defensive tactics; and the fundamental laws of human nature: these are things that must most certainly be studied."

- Sun Tzu

People don't behave according to potential, words, or intentions. They behave according to what is rewarded and what is tolerated. Terrain matters. Context matters. Stakes matter. If the environment rewards minimal effort, you'll get minimal effort. If confusion is allowed to persist, it will. Strategy isn't cruelty, it's realism. Study incentives and you stop personalizing behavior that was never personal in the first place.

Depth bonds, avoidance fractures.

"When invading hostile territory, the general principle is, that penetrating deeply brings cohesion; penetrating but a short way means dispersion."

- Sun Tzu

Shallow terrain produces drift. No structure, no stakes, no reason to anchor. But depth changes people. Real investment creates

104

cohesion unless someone is wired to flee it. When emotional territory deepens, secure people attach more fully. Avoidant people fragment, pull back, or destabilize the bond. This isn't about timing or chemistry. It's about capacity. Depth reveals architecture.

The danger zone of almost.

"When you leave your own country behind, and take your army across neighborhood territory, you find yourself on critical ground. When there are means of communication on all four sides, the ground is one of intersecting highways."

- Sun Tzu

That weird zone where you're not home, not deep, but invested enough to get hurt. That's where most women get played.

Stop treating shallow like serious.

"When you penetrate deeply into a country, it is serious ground. When you penetrate but a little way, it is facile ground."

- Sun Tzu

Early access, vague plans, inconsistent effort, late-night intimacy, and "seeing where it goes" are not depth. They are proximity without commitment. Serious ground has weight. It has structure, risk, and consequence. It requires presence, planning, and follow-through.

When you treat shallow like serious, you over-invest, over-interpret, and over-attach to something that was never built to hold you. Depth earns seriousness. Anything less is just convenient access wearing a serious face.

When staying costs your soul.

"When you have the enemy's strongholds on your rear, and narrow passes in front, it is hemmed-in ground. When there is no place of refuge at all, it is desperate ground."

- Sun Tzu

Hemmed-in ground is when leaving feels expensive. You've invested time, sex, hope, reputation, maybe even a toothbrush. The exits are narrow, uncomfortable, and emotionally costly, so you keep telling yourself to "wait it out."

Desperate ground is when staying costs more than leaving ever could. That's when your self-respect is leaking. Your nervous system is fried. You're shrinking, negotiating, rationalizing behavior you would roast a friend for tolerating.

Hemmed-in feels scary. Desperate feels suffocating. And here's the part no one likes to admit: most women don't leave on hemmed-in ground. They wait until it becomes desperate ground. Until their soul starts filing formal complaints. If staying requires you to abandon who you are, that's not loyalty. That's entrapment with good lighting.

THE SECOND LIST OF WHAT TO DO
Unify your purpose.

"Therefore, on dispersive ground, I would inspire my men with unity of purpose. On facile ground, I would see that there is close connection between all parts of my army."

-     Sun Tzu

Dispersive ground is where you feel *comfortable.*
Familiar. Nostalgic. Emotionally "at home."

That's exactly where women scatter. You start multitasking emotionally: hoping, explaining, excusing, negotiating, over-functioning. Your standards fracture. One part of you wants dignity, another part wants reassurance, another part just wants the anxiety to stop.

That's how power leaks. Unity of purpose means you stop letting every feeling vote. You choose one governing objective and let it run the whole operation. That objective is not love.

It's not chemistry. It's not potential. It's self-respect. When self-respect is the command center, your actions align. Your boundaries stop wobbling. Your energy stops contradicting itself. You stop sending mixed signals because you're no longer mixed inside. A unified woman is hard to manipulate, impossible to rush, and very expensive to waste.

Don't isolate early.

"On contentious ground, I would hurry up my rear."

- Sun Tzu

Contentious ground is early dating where *stakes are forming but trust is not*.

This is the danger zone. Isolation here is not romance. It's tactical failure. When you collapse your world into one man too early, you lose perspective, leverage, and supply lines. Friends go quiet. Routines slip. Your calendar opens up "coincidentally." Suddenly his mood controls the temperature of your entire life.

That's how women get negotiated downward.

"Hurrying up your rear" means reinforcing what's behind you before you advance. Your rear is your support system: friends, work, goals, therapy, gym, sleep, identity. These are not distractions. They are armor. Early attachment without reinforcement makes you vulnerable to:

- accepting inconsistency
- rationalizing disrespect
- mistaking intensity for intimacy
- overvaluing access because it feels scarce

A woman who stays socially and emotionally connected moves differently. She asks clearer questions. She waits longer. She doesn't panic when there's silence.

If a connection is real, it will survive you having a life. If it collapses because you didn't disappear into him, it was never safe terrain to begin with. Isolation is how wars are lost.

Bring your standards with you.

"On open ground, I would keep a vigilant eye on my defenses. On ground of intersecting highways, I would consolidate my alliances."

- Sun Tzu

Open ground is where access is easy. Texts flow. Plans are vague. Energy is friendly but undefined. This is exactly where women drop their defenses because nothing *bad* has happened yet. But open ground is not safe ground. It's exposed ground.

Keeping an eye on your defenses means you don't relax your standards just because things feel light, fun, or promising. You don't outsource judgment to chemistry. You don't assume intention where none has been demonstrated.

Intersecting ground is where multiple influences cross: his friends, his exes, his habits, your hopes, outside opinions, your past patterns. This is where people get confused and pulled in different directions. So, you consolidate alliances.

That means you keep your logic online, your friends in the loop, and your values non-negotiable. You reality-check instead of romanticize. You let trusted voices ground you instead of isolating inside your own feelings.

Arriving emotionally alone makes you easy to sway. Arriving with standards, context, and support makes you stable.

You don't win by being open-hearted and undefended. You win by being open-eyed and well-supported.

Observe openly, verify socially.

> *"On serious ground, I would try to ensure a continuous stream of supplies. On difficult ground, I would keep pushing on along the road."*
>
> - Sun Tzu

Serious ground is when emotional stakes are real. Feelings are forming. Time is invested. Consequences now exist. At this stage, you don't run on hope. You secure supplies.

In dating, your supplies are consistency, communication, effort, and support. If those are intermittent, you don't push deeper.

You stabilize first. No steady supply line means no forward movement.

Difficult ground is when logistics, timing, distance, or complexity make things harder. This is not the moment to stop and "wait it out." Waiting here drains energy and clarity.

You either keep moving with structure and momentum, or you exit. What you don't do is confuse difficulty with destiny.

Progress without supplies is delusion. Supplies without progress is stagnation. Both are losing positions. On open ground, observe for consistency. On intersecting ground, protect reputation and get reality checks.

Choose a real plan.

"On hemmed-in ground, I would block any way of retreat. On desperate ground, I would proclaim to my soldiers the hopelessness of saving their lives."

- Sun Tzu

There are stages where softness is wisdom. This is not one of them.

Serious ground: Protect your health, your money, and your sanity first. If any of those are being eroded, you are no longer "seeing how it goes." You are bleeding.

Difficult ground: Do not stall. Hesitation here is not caution, it's avoidance disguised as patience. Waiting for clarity that never arrives is how people lose years.

Hemmed-in ground: This is where most women lie to themselves. You keep imaginary exits alive:

- *"Maybe he'll change."*
- *"Maybe I'm overreacting."*
- *"Maybe if I just…"*

No. Hemmed-in ground requires one ruthless move: kill the escape fantasies. Choose a real plan, forward or out. Anything else is self-betrayal.

Desperate ground: This is the point of no illusion. You stop pretending there is a version of this where you survive *inside* the fire. You name the truth plainly. You act decisively. You save yourself without asking permission.

Sun Tzu didn't motivate soldiers here. He woke them up. So will you.

WHY THIS WORKS
Pressure reveals truth.

"For it is the soldier's disposition to offer an obstinate resistance when surrounded, to fight hard when he cannot help himself, and to obey promptly when he has fallen into danger."

- Sun Tzu

When you stop giving yourself emotional exits, you stop negotiating with trash.

ALLIES + GUIDES
Choose guides, not narratives.

"We cannot enter into alliance with neighboring princes until we are acquainted with their designs. We are not fit to lead an army on the march unless we are familiar with the face of the country—its mountains and forests, its pitfalls and precipices, its marshes and swamps. We shall be unable to turn natural advantages to account unless we make use of local guides."

- Sun Tzu

Don't trust his friends, his ex-story, his "I'm a good guy" PR.

Know the terrain: his habits, patterns, lifestyle.
Use guides: trusted friends, therapist, your own data.

Refusal to learn guarantees repetition.

"To be ignorant of any one of the following four or five principles does not befit a warlike prince."

- Sun Tzu

Translation: if you refuse to learn, dating will keep teaching you the same lesson with different faces.

HOW TO TAKE DOWN A POWERFUL STATE
Refuse triangulation.

"When a warlike prince attacks a powerful state, his generalship shows itself in preventing the concentration of the enemy's forces. He overawes his opponents, and their allies are prevented from joining against him."

- Sun Tzu

Triangulation is when a man never deals with you directly. Instead, he routes the dynamic through: exes, other women, "my friends think…," stories about attention he's getting, comparisons you didn't ask for. This isn't transparency. It's leverage.

Triangulation keeps you off-balance. It forces you to compete, explain, or self-correct against invisible opponents. The moment you react to any of it, you're no longer dealing with *him*, you're fighting ghosts. Refusing triangulation means this:

- You do not engage with third-party opinions.
- You do not compete with unnamed women.
- You do not defend yourself against people who aren't in the room.
- You collapse the triangle into a line.

If he wants something, he states it. If there's a concern, it comes directly from him. If he can't stand on his own position without backup, commentary, or comparison, he is not ready to engage you. A strong position does not need allies. A weak one hides behind them. Force the line or exit the field.

111

Execute standards quietly.

"Hence, he does not strive to ally himself with all and sundry, nor does he foster the power of other states. He carries out his own secret designs, keeping his antagonists in awe. Thus, he is able to capture their cities and overthrow their kingdoms."

- Sun Tzu

Standards lose power when they're announced. The moment you explain them, justify them, or crowdsource them, they become negotiable. You turn boundaries into talking points and invite debate where none is required.

Stop recruiting a committee for your dating life. Friends, therapists, group chats, and the man himself do not get a vote on what you tolerate.

Quiet execution looks like this:
- You don't warn.
- You don't threaten.
- You don't deliver speeches.
- You simply remove access.

Absence is the consequence. Consistency is the message. Silence is the enforcement. A woman who executes standards quietly doesn't need to convince anyone she's serious. The outcome speaks for her.

REWARDS + ORDERS + CONTROL
Reward consistency, not crumbs.

"Bestow rewards without regard to rule, issue orders without regard to previous arrangements; and you will be able to handle a whole army as though you had to do with but a single man."

- Sun Tzu

Stop being predictable:
- don't reward breadcrumbs
- reward consistency
- adjust in real time when new info arrives

Silence is strategy.

"Confront your soldiers with the deed itself; never let them know your design. When the outlook is bright, bring it before their eyes; but tell them nothing when the situation is gloomy."

- Sun Tzu

If it's good, let it be seen.

If it's bad, don't debate it into "maybe."

Silence is strategy.

DEADLY PERIL CREATES SURVIVAL

Consequence creates growth.

"Place your army in deadly peril, and it will survive; plunge it into desperate straits, and it will come off in safety."

- Sun Tzu

Growth does not come from comfort. It comes from consequence. As long as someone is protected from the cost of their behavior, nothing changes. Effort stays minimal. Patterns repeat. Potential rots.

Your glow-up doesn't begin when you try harder. It begins when you stop cushioning the impact.

No more soft landings. No more emotional subsidies. No more staying "nice" to avoid discomfort. When access is removed, reality hits. When consequences are real, adaptation follows. This applies to men and to you.

The moment you allow things to fall apart instead of holding them together, strength appears. Standards sharpen. Self-respect consolidates.

Sun Tzu didn't save his army by easing the danger. He saved them by letting the stakes wake them up. So, stop rescuing outcomes. Let consequence do what comfort never could.

Pain sharpens action.

"For it is precisely when a force has fallen into harm's way that is capable of striking a blow for victory."

- Sun Tzu

Pain is not the problem. Avoiding it is. Pain strips illusion. It collapses indecision. It forces movement where comfort allowed delay. When something hurts enough, the mind stops negotiating and starts acting. That's why clarity often arrives after heartbreak, humiliation, or loss not before. Use it.

Don't numb it. Don't romanticize it. Don't wait for it to pass. Let pain compress your choices until only the true ones remain. Cut what's unsustainable. End what's dishonest. Move where you've been hesitating.

Pain is the moment the fog lifts. Action is what turns it into victory. Waste the pain and you repeat the lesson. Use it and you don't need it again.

ACCOMMODATE THE ENEMY'S PURPOSE
Outmaneuver incentives.

"Success in warfare is gained by carefully accommodating ourselves to the enemy's purpose."

- Sun Tzu

Dating translation: learn his incentives so you can outmaneuver, not plead. If he wants casual, don't argue. Exit or restructure the terrain.

Stay near the weak points.

"By persistently hanging on the enemy's flank, we shall succeed in the long run in killing the commander-in-chief."

- Sun Tzu

Stay consistent near the weak points: his inconsistency, his ego, his avoidance. Time reveals lies.

Strategy beats persuasion.

"This is called ability to accomplish a thing by sheer cunning."

-    Sun Tzu

Persuasion tries to change people. Strategy changes conditions. Persuasion argues, explains, convinces, and waits for agreement. Strategy assumes people will remain exactly who they are and adjusts accordingly. This isn't manipulation. It's realism.

You don't talk a storm into calming down. You don't reason someone into consistency. You don't negotiate attraction, effort, or character. You build shelter. That means boundaries instead of debates. Positioning instead of pleading. Action instead of explanation.

When the environment changes, behavior follows. When you stop persuading and start positioning, outcomes resolve themselves. Strategy doesn't beg the weather to cooperate. It prepares for reality and stays standing when others get soaked.

COMMAND DAY RULES

Cut power leaks.

"On the day that you take up your command, block the frontier passes, destroy the official tallies, and stop the passage of all emissaries."

-    Sun Tzu

Cut channels that leak your power: late-night texting, "checking in," stalking, mutual friends relaying messages.

Decide privately, move once.

"Be stern in the council-chamber, so that you may control the situation."

-    Sun Tzu

All real decisions are made in private. If you're still debating, polling friends, testing reactions, or half-moving to see what happens, you haven't decided. And half-decisions create chaos, mixed signals, and regret.

Sun Tzu was clear: command happens before action. That means you decide internally without him watching, without feedback, without emotional interference. You ratify the choice with

115

yourself first. Once the decision is made, there is no rehearsal, no announcement, no wobbling.

Then you move. Once.
No backtracking.
No "checking in."
No re-explaining the decision because guilt showed up late.

Power isn't loud. It's clean. The person who decides privately and moves decisively controls the situation not because they're forceful, but because they're finished.

OPEN DOOR + WHAT HE HOLDS DEAR
Respond to real openings.

> *"If the enemy leaves a door open, you must rush in."*
>
> - Sun Tzu

If he shows real opening: accountability, clarity, effort, respond quickly. Don't punish growth.

Control access and timing.

> *"Forestall your opponent by seizing what he holds dear, and subtly contrive to time his arrival on the ground."*
>
> - Sun Tzu

Access is leverage. Timing is the multiplier. You don't gain power by being endlessly available. You gain it by deciding who gets access, when, and at what pace. Attention, intimacy, emotional availability, all of it is currency.

But restraint alone isn't strategy. If you wait too long to act, to leave, to advance, to set a boundary, the moment passes. Leverage expires. Clarity closes. Control access and move while the opening exists.

Don't linger hoping timing will fix hesitation. Don't arrive late to the moment that required decisiveness. Power isn't just about withholding. It's about recognizing when the window is open and stepping through it cleanly.

116

RULES VS CANONS
Rules first, tactics flexible.

"Walk in the path defined by rule, and accommodate yourself to the enemy until you can fight a decisive battle."

- Sun Tzu

Your rules do not change. Your tactics must. Rules are your non-negotiables: standards, values, what you require to stay. They are fixed. They do not bend for chemistry, timing, or potential.

Tactics are everything else: how much you speak, when you pull back, how available you are, what you reward, what you ignore. Confusing the two is how people rationalize staying too long. You adapt tactics to gather information and maintain position not to lower the bar. You stay fluid only until the moment becomes clear.

Every situation moves toward one decisive outcome: commitment or exit. If your rules stay intact, the decision is clean. If your rules erode, no tactic will save you. Flexibility without standards is drift. Standards without flexibility is rigidity. Master both and you control the outcome.

THE MAIDEN + RUNNING HARE
Observe first, then move fast.

"At first, then, exhibit the coyness of a maiden, until the enemy gives you an opening; afterwards emulate the rapidity of a running hare, and it will be too late for the enemy to oppose you."

- Sun Tzu

Dating translation: Don't reveal your whole heart at first contact. Observe. Collect data. Let him show his hand. Then when the opening appears, move fast: define, commit, or cut.

CHAPTER 12

THE ATTACK BY FIRE
Burn the Fantasy.

Dating apps are a theater built to keep you hope-drunk. This chapter is how you stop politely dying in it. Fire, in Sun Tzŭ terms, is controlled destruction. In dating, fire is cutting off the fuel source.

THE FIVE FIRES

Fire One: Burn the soldiers in their camp
Translation: don't argue with the man. Destroy the environment where he keeps winning. Block, unmatch, remove access, stop "just checking."
You're not trying to convert him. You're trying to end the campaign.

Fire Two: Burn the stores
Translation: burn his resupply.
The stores are: your attention, forgiveness, late-night emotional labor, "I miss you" texts, sexual access, your empathy.

Fire Three: Burn the baggage trains
Translation: burn the history that keeps dragging you back.
Photos, old texts, playlists, the "good memories," the screenshots you reread to justify staying.

Fire Four: Burn the arsenals and magazines
Translation: burn his weapons.

His weapons are: ambiguity, future-faking, word salad, guilt trips, "you're crazy," hot-cold cycles, pity stories, trauma dumping as a leash.

Fire Five: Drop fire into the enemy

Translation: strategic exposure to reality. Not public humiliation. Reality.

Examples: "I'm dating intentionally. If you're not, I'm out." Or: "I don't do casual."

Fire = clarity that forces a reveal.

HAVE YOUR FIRE KIT READY

"In order to carry out an attack, we must have means available. the material for raising fire should always be kept in readiness."

- Sun Tzu

Translation: You can't burn a fantasy if you don't have tools. Your dating fire kit:

- A clean boundary script
- A block/unmatch plan (all platforms)
- A no-contact rule (timeboxed if you need)
- A friend / therapist / accountability buddy
- Replacement rituals: gym, work sprint, social plans, sleep

WAIT FOR THE WIND

"There is a proper season for making attacks with fire, and special days for starting a conflagration. The proper season is when the weather is very dry; the special days are those when the moon is in the constellations of the Sieve, the Wall, the Wing or the Cross-bar; for these four are all days of rising wind."

- Sun Tzu

Sun Tzŭ: dry weather and windy days.

Dating: when you're emotionally "dry" enough to act and the truth is "windy" enough to spread.

Best season to burn the fantasy:
- right after a disrespect
- right after a lie
- right after ghosting
- right after your nervous system finally says "enough"

That's your wind. Use it.

WHAT HAPPENS AFTER YOU SET A BOUNDARY

Sun Tzu treats fire as a forcing function. Once fire is introduced, the situation *will* change. The mistake is reacting emotionally instead of recognizing which phase you're in.

When you set a real boundary, you ignite the terrain. These are the five possible developments and how to respond.

EXPECT FIVE DEVELOPMENTS

""In attacking with fire, one should be prepared to meet five possible developments."

- Sun Tzu

Once a boundary is set, the dynamic *evolves*. Nothing stays neutral. Your job is not to panic or explain, it's to identify the development and act accordingly.

1) Fire breaks inside his camp, attack from outside

"When fire breaks out inside the enemy's camp, respond at once with an attack from without."

- Sun Tzu

Translation: If he starts spiraling, lying, double-booking, acting shady, or unraveling after the boundary, do not step inside to fix it.

120

That chaos is internal. Your move is external.

Attack from outside = remove access.
Do not soothe the fire you didn't start.

2) Fire Breaks Out, but He Stays Quiet → Hold

"If there is an outbreak of fire, but the enemy's soldiers remain quiet, bide your time and do not attack."

- Sun Tzu

Translation: If you set a boundary and he stays calm, unfazed, or silent, do not charge. This is not indifference. It's preparedness. He is waiting you out. So, you wait without blinking.

3) When Flames Peak → Act if Practical, Otherwise Hold the Line

"When the force of the flames has reached its height, follow it up with an attack, if that is practicable; if not, stay where you are."

- Sun Tzu

Translation: When the truth becomes obvious — patterns undeniable, behavior consistent — move if you can.

If circumstances don't yet allow a clean exit, hold the line. Do not negotiate inside the smoke. Smoke distorts judgment.

4) If Fire Can Be Started From Outside → Do Not Wait

"If it is possible to make an assault with fire from without, do not wait for it to break out within."

- Sun Tzu

Translation: Do not wait for proof. Do not wait for closure. Do not wait for him to admit anything. If the terrain is combustible, if the pattern is already clear, act now. Waiting is how leverage expires.

5) Be to Windward

"When you start a fire, be to windward of it. Do not attack from the leeward."

- Sun Tzu

Translation: Never set or enforce boundaries from weakness.

Windward: calm, resourced, grounded, prepared.
Leeward: panicking, lonely, horny, seeking validation, trying to "win him."

If you're leeward, don't act yet. Stabilize first, then move.

FINAL DOCTRINE

Fire is not drama. Fire is information. Once it's lit, do not jump into it. Read it. Position yourself correctly. Then act once, cleanly. That's the doctrine.

DON'T BURN AT NIGHT

"A wind that rises in the daytime lasts long, but a night breeze soon falls."

- Sun Tzu

Translation: don't launch the burn at 1:00 a.m.
Night wind is emotional, impulsive, romantic.
Day wind is sober, decisive, clean.

EXPECT THE BACKSLIDE

"In every army, the five developments connected with fire must be known, the movements of the stars calculated, and a watch kept for the proper days."

- Sun Tzu

Translation: anticipate his counterattacks:
- lovebombing after disrespect
- "I miss you" after you detach
- rage when you enforce consequences
- fake apology with zero repair
- sudden "commitment" when you leave

Plan for it so you don't fold.

END IT OR DRAG IT OUT

"Hence those who use fire as an aid to the attack show intelligence; those who use water as an aid to the attack gain an accession of strength. By means of water, an enemy may be intercepted, but not robbed of all his belongings."

- Sun Tzu

Fire ends the war. Water only blocks the road.

Dating translation:
- Fire = cut the cord. remove fuel. end access.
- Water = slow it down. mute him. distance. "I'm busy."

Water helps, but it doesn't destroy the fantasy. Fire does.

CHANGE REQUIRES A BOLD MOVE

"Unhappy is the fate of one who tries to win his battles and succeed in his attacks without cultivating the spirit of enterprise; for the result is waste of time and general stagnation. Hence the saying: The enlightened ruler lays his plans well ahead; the good general cultivates his resources."

- Sun Tzu

Unhappy is the one who wants victory without bold action.

Translation: if you want a different love life, you need at least one heroic move. Ending what you keep tolerating.

The enlightened ruler plans ahead.

Translation: don't wait until you're in emotional withdrawal to decide your rules. Decide now.

DON'T ENGAGE WITHOUT A WIN

"Move not unless you see an advantage; use not your troops unless there is something to be gained; fight not unless the position is critical."

- Sun Tzu

Translation: Don't send paragraphs. Don't "check in." Don't do the closure coffee. Move only if it gains you clarity, safety, or resolution.

123

DON'T EXIT TO PROVE A POINT

"No ruler should put troops into the field merely to gratify his own spleen; no general should fight a battle simply out of pique."

\- Sun Tzu

No ruler sends troops out of spleen.

Translation: Don't block as a performance. Don't exit to punish. Exit to protect your future.

IF IT HELPS YOU, ACT. IF NOT, WAIT.

"If it is to your advantage, make a forward move; if not, stay where you are."

\- Sun Tzu

This rule is simple and constantly ignored. Before you text, explain, confront, meet, or "check in," ask one question: What do I gain by moving right now? Advantage in dating is not emotional relief. It's clarity, safety, dignity, or resolution.

If your move:

- clarifies the situation
- protects your boundaries
- ends confusion
- or removes you from harm

You act.

If your move only:

- soothes anxiety
- chases reassurance
- keeps a dead dynamic alive
- or reopens a door you already closed

You hold.

Stillness is not avoidance when nothing is gained by action. It is discipline.

124

Most women don't lose because they waited too long. They lose because they moved when the move served their feelings not their future.

FEELINGS PASS. DAMAGE LASTS.

"Anger may in time change to gladness; vexation may be succeeded by content. But a kingdom that has once been destroyed can never come again into being; nor can the dead ever be brought back to life. Hence the enlightened ruler is heedful, and the good general full of caution. This is the way to keep a country at peace and an army intact."

- Sun Tzu

Your feelings will change. Your time won't come back.

Translation:

- your rage will soften
- your loneliness will spike
- your nostalgia will lie

But the cost of staying stacks permanently.

So, the enlightened ruler is cautious.
The good general protects the army.
Translation: protect you.

Your "Burn the Fantasy" Rules

1. If it costs your peace, it's combustible.
2. Don't negotiate in smoke.
3. Burn access first. Explanations later.
4. Boundaries are not debates.
5. If you need proof, you're already losing time.

CHAPTER 13

THE USE OF SPIES
Recon, Receipts, and Pattern Recognition on Dating Apps

DATING WITHOUT INTELLIGENCE IS EXPENSIVE

"Raising a host of a hundred thousand men and marching them great distances entails heavy loss on the people and a drain on the resources of the State. The daily expenditure will amount to a thousand ounces of silver. There will be commotion at home and abroad, and men will drop down exhausted on the highways. As many as seven hundred thousand families will be impeded in their labor."

- Sun Tzu

Raising emotional armies, investing months, traveling across cities, buying outfits, therapy sessions, "just one more conversation," and emotional labor will bankrupt you faster than war ever bankrupted a state.

Men drop off.
Women burn out.
Everyone's exhausted on the emotional highway wondering where it went wrong.

That's what happens when you date blind.

LONG WARS ARE FOUGHT BECAUSE WOMEN IGNORE EARLY DATA

"Hostile armies may face each other for years, striving for the victory which is decided in a single day. This being so, to remain in ignorance of the enemy's condition simply because one grudges the outlay of a hundred ounces of silver in honors and emoluments, is the height of inhumanity."

- Sun Tzu

Situationships don't last years because love is complicated. They last years because someone ignored the first six red flags and called it "potential."

To refuse to gather information early because you "don't want to seem paranoid" is not romantic. It is strategic negligence.

IF YOU WON'T GATHER INFORMATION, EXPECT CONFUSION

"One who acts thus is no leader of men, no present help to his sovereign, no master of victory."

- Sun Tzu

If you refuse to observe, verify, cross-check, and quietly collect information:
- You are not intuitive.
- You are not "going with the flow."
- You are volunteering to be confused.

WOMEN WHO SEE EARLY DON'T LOSE

"Thus, what enables the wise sovereign and the good general to strike and conquer, and achieve things beyond the reach of ordinary men, is foreknowledge."

- Sun Tzu

The women who win at dating don't "try harder."

They see earlier. They don't guess intent. They observe behavior.

YOU CAN'T MANIFEST CONSISTENCY

"Now this foreknowledge cannot be elicited from spirits; it cannot be obtained inductively from experience, nor by any deductive calculation."

- Sun Tzu

Intuition tells you when something feels off.
It does not turn inconsistency into reliability.

You cannot intuition your way around:
- inconsistent effort
- emotional avoidance
- patterned dishonesty

No amount of manifestation, patience, or "trusting the process" will stabilize behavior that isn't there. Vibes are signals. Patterns are proof.

Use intuition to notice the problem. Use evidence to decide.

TRUTH COMES FROM PATTERNS, NOT PROMISES

"Knowledge of the enemy's dispositions can only be obtained from other men."

- Sun Tzu

Profiles lie.
Words lie.
Men lie.

Patterns don't. Screenshots don't. Receipts don't.

PAY ATTENTION LIKE A GROWN WOMAN
THE FIVE DATING SPIES

"Hence the use of spies, of whom there are five classes: Local spies; inward spies; converted spies; doomed spies; surviving spies."

- Sun Tzu

This does **not** mean stalking. It means observing reality without flinching. These are the five ways truth reveals itself in dating.

1. Local Spies (His Environment Tells on Him)

"Having local spies means employing the services of the inhabitants of a district."

- Sun Tzu

Local spies are the surroundings. His lifestyle. His routines. His friends. His relationship history. The way people around him behave.

You learn who a man is by the world he maintains. Chaos leaves residue. Stability does too. If his environment contradicts his words, believe the environment.

2. Inward Spies (He Tells on Himself)

"Having inward spies, making use of officials of the enemy."

- Sun Tzu

Inward spies are his own behavior. Consistency. Follow-through. Tone shifts. What changes when you set a boundary. You don't interrogate. You watch. People reveal their character naturally when they think they're safe to be themselves.

3. Converted Spies (Patterns From the Past #HisOwnWords)

"Having converted spies, getting hold of the enemy's spies and using them for our own purposes."

- Sun Tzu

Converted spies are information that flips once pressure is applied. Old stories that don't line up. Explanations that change over time. Exes who were "all crazy" in identical ways.

Patterns eventually defect from the narrative and tell the truth. You don't need every detail. You need repetition.

Men always tell on themselves. You just have to stop interrupting. When his words change depending on the audience, he's not evolving, he's adapting.

129

4. Doomed Spies (How He Acts When He Thinks He's Losing You)

"Having doomed spies, doing certain things openly for purposes of deception, and allowing our own spies to know of them and report them to the enemy."

- Sun Tzu

Doomed spies are revealed under consequence.

Watch what happens when: you pull back, you say no, you stop overgiving, access is threatened.

Sometimes you let him think:
- You believe him
- You're fine with ambiguity
- You didn't notice

Entitlement, rage, panic, lovebombing, or sudden commitment attempts appear here. That's not manipulation. That's confirmation.

5. Surviving Spies (What Remains Over Time)

"Surviving spies, finally, are those who bring back news from the enemy's camp."

- Sun Tzu

Surviving spies are what holds up after time passes.

Who is still consistent when the novelty wears off?
Who stays respectful without chasing?
Who doesn't disappear once effort is required?

Time eliminates performance. What survives is real.

Final Truth

You don't need to spy on a man. You need to stop ignoring what's visible. When all five are observed together, the fantasy collapses on its own. No confrontation. No drama. No guessing. Just clarity. That's grown-woman strategy.

WHEN YOU SEE EVERYTHING, THE FANTASY DIES

"When these five kinds of spy are all at work, none can discover the secret system. This is called "divine manipulation of the threads." It is the sovereign's most precious faculty."

- Sun Tzu

This is called *divine manipulation of the threads*. Or, in modern terms: He cannot bullshit you anymore.

GUARD THESE OBSERVATIONS CLOSELY

"Hence it is that with none in the whole army are more intimate relations to be maintained than with spies. None should be more liberally rewarded. In no other business should greater secrecy be preserved."

- Sun Tzu

Do not over-share your intel with friends who romanticize crumbs. Do not confront too early. Do not announce your conclusions. Information is power. Silence keeps it intact.

YOU NEED INTUITION *AND* DISCERNMENT

"Spies cannot be usefully employed without a certain intuitive sagacity."

- Sun Tzu

Intuition without verification is how women end up crying over men who "felt different."

Pattern recognition is intuition with receipts.

YOU MUST BE CALM TO READ THE TRUTH

"They cannot be properly managed without benevolence and straightforwardness."

- Sun Tzu

Anxious women miss signals. Emotionally regulated women see everything. Stillness sharpens perception.

131

CLEVER MEN WILL TRY TO BLUR THE PATTERN

"Without subtle ingenuity of mind, one cannot make certain of the truth of their reports."

-   Sun Tzu

When patterns start to form, clever men don't deny them. They muddy them. They reframe. They minimize. They introduce just enough doubt to make you question your memory, your instincts, your timeline. This is gaslighting not always loud, often polite.

Confusion is not accidental. It's a tactic to keep you debating instead of deciding. The moment you start explaining what you *meant*, defending how you *felt*, or rehashing what already happened, the pattern has done its job. Clarity ends games. Patterns end arguments. And the woman who stops negotiating reality cannot be played.

BE SUBTLE

"Be subtle! be subtle! and use your spies for every kind of business."

-   Sun Tzu

You do not need to announce you're clocking him.
You don't need to accuse.
You don't need to explain.
You just… adjust.

IF THE TRUTH LEAKS TOO EARLY, YOU LOSE THE UPPER HAND

"If a secret piece of news is divulged by a spy before the time is ripe, he must be put to death together with the man to whom the secret was told."

-   Sun Tzu

Confrontation before certainty creates chaos. Let the pattern finish forming. Patterns always complete themselves.

START WITH HIS INFRASTRUCTURE

"Whether the object be to crush an army, to storm a city, or to assassinate an individual, it is always necessary to begin by finding out the names of the attendants, the aides-de- camp, the door-keepers and sentries of the general in command. Our spies must be commissioned to ascertain these."

- Sun Tzu

Who does he talk to? Who has access? Who knows his schedule? Who runs interference? That's where the truth leaks from.

WHEN HIS STORIES COLLAPSE, EVERYTHING ELSE FOLLOWS

"The enemy's spies who have come to spy on us must be sought out, tempted with bribes, led away and comfortably housed. Thus they will become converted spies and available for our service."

- Sun Tzu

Once one lie breaks, the entire narrative follows. You don't have to dismantle it. Gravity will.

ALL INTELLIGENCE FEEDS ALL OTHERS

"It is through the information brought by the converted spy that we are able to acquire and employ local and inward spies."

- Sun Tzu

One inconsistency reveals three more. One excuse reveals five patterns. This is why women say: "I don't know why, but something feels off."

Your subconscious already ran the data.

INTELLIGENCE IS THE ENTIRE POINT

"It is owing to his information, again, that we can cause the doomed spy to carry false tidings to the enemy."

- Sun Tzu

The goal is not to catch him in a lie. It's not to corner him, confront him, or win an argument. The goal is to see clearly enough to disengage early.

Information gives you leverage, but clarity gives you freedom. When you understand the pattern, you don't need proof, permission, or confession. You simply stop investing. You don't expose him. You exit clean. That's intelligence not drama.

SPYING IS NOT PARANOIA

"Lastly, it is by his information that the surviving spy can be used on appointed occasions."

- Sun Tzu

It is respect for your time, body, and emotional resources.
Men who are honest never feel threatened by observation.

THE CONVERTED SPY IS THE KEY

"The end and aim of spying in all its five varieties is knowledge of the enemy; and this knowledge can only be derived, in the first instance, from the converted spy. Hence it is essential that the converted spy be treated with the utmost liberality."

- Sun Tzu

The moment his story starts contradicting itself, the truth has surfaced. Details change. Timelines shift. Explanations multiply. That's not complexity. That's a narrative collapsing under pressure.

When this happens, you don't interrogate. You don't demand clarification. You don't help him reconcile the story. You mark the moment and you stop advancing. Contradiction is the converted spy. Once it speaks, you already have what you need.

EMPIRES FALL BECAUSE INSIDERS KNOW TOO MUCH

"Of old, the rise of the Yin dynasty was due to I Chih who had served under the Hsia. Likewise, the rise of the Chou dynasty was due to Lü Ya who had served under the Yin."

- Sun Tzu

Men lose control of narratives when women stop idealizing and start observing. Every downfall starts with a woman seeing clearly.

DATING WITHOUT PATTERN RECOGNITION IS DATING BLIND

"Hence it is only the enlightened ruler and the wise general who will use the highest intelligence of the army for purposes of spying and thereby they achieve great results. Spies are a most important element in war, because on them depends an army's ability to move."

- Sun Tzu

An army without spies is deaf and blind.

A woman without pattern recognition is trusting vibes in a hostile system.

FINAL TRUTH

Spies are not about suspicion.
They are about clarity.

And clarity is what keeps you from burning years of your life on men who were never serious to begin with.

EPILOGUE

Peace Is the Point

If you read this book all the way through, I want you to understand something: This was never about staying in fight mode. Strategy is not a personality. It's a phase.

You learn it so you don't keep paying for the same lesson. You study patterns so you don't romanticize confusion. You sharpen discernment so you don't confuse anxiety with chemistry ever again.

The goal was never to win men. The goal was to stop losing yourself. Peace is not boring. It's stable. It's safe. It's quiet in a way that lets you hear your own thoughts again.

When strategy works, dating stops feeling like a battlefield and starts feeling like a filter. The wrong people disqualify themselves quickly. The right ones don't require tactics at all. Eventually, you won't need this book. That's the success metric. You'll notice sooner. Leave faster. Recover cleaner. Trust yourself more.

And one day, you'll look back at the version of you who stayed too long and feel tenderness not shame. She did the best she could with what she knew at the time.

Now you know more. Put the armor down. Keep the wisdom. Choose peace early, often, and without apology. That's the real victory.

RED FLAGS VS TERRAIN

Why Not Every Bad Feeling Means "Bad Man"

Not every red flag is a villain. Sometimes it's just the wrong landscape. A red flag is a behavior. Terrain is the environment that makes behavior inevitable. Confusing the two is how women personalize outcomes that were never about them.

RED FLAGS

Red flags are actions that would be a problem anywhere.

Lying. Chronic inconsistency. Defensiveness around accountability. Disappearing acts. Weaponized vulnerability.

These don't improve with time, patience, or better communication. They follow the person.

TERRAIN

Terrain is context.

Timing. Life phase. Emotional capacity. Lifestyle mismatch. Competing priorities.

A man can be decent and still unavailable. He can like you and still be incapable of showing up. That doesn't make him evil, it makes the terrain uninhabitable.

WHY THIS DISTINCTION MATTERS

If it's a red flag, you exit.
If it's terrain, you stop trying to adapt yourself to it.

What you don't do is:
- work harder to fix the land
- negotiate with reality
- shrink to fit a place that can't sustain you

You don't build a home on a floodplain and call it love.

THE TRAP

Women often stay because the man isn't "that bad."
But dating is not a morality contest.

You don't need a villain to leave. You need incompatibility. And terrain never changes because you want it to.

FINAL TRUTH

Red flags tell you who he is.
Terrain tells you where you are.

Both are information.
Neither is a challenge.

Your job is not to endure the landscape.
It's to choose one that lets you thrive.

That's not being picky.
That's being strategic.

THE ULTIMATE CHEAT SHEET

1. STRATEGY IS NOT MANIPULATION

Strategy is self-command.
Manipulation tries to change him.
Strategy decides *you*.

2. SELF-COMMAND COMES FIRST

If you are anxious, spiraling, bargaining, or attached to outcome, do not move. Regulate first. No clean decision is made from panic.

3. RULES ARE FIXED. TACTICS ARE FLEXIBLE

Your standards don't change. Your timing, silence, and pacing can. If your rules erode, no tactic will save you.

4. DON'T ARRIVE EMOTIONALLY ALONE

Bring your logic, your friends, your routines, your reality. Isolation is how fantasies survive.

5. HAVE YOUR FIRE KIT READY

Never set a boundary without:
- an exit plan
- a no-contact rule
- support
- replacement rituals

Hope is not a plan.

6. WAIT FOR THE WIND

Act when:
- disrespect appears
- lies surface
- ghosting happens
- your nervous system says "enough"

Do not burn at 1 a.m. Night feelings lie.

7. CONTROL ACCESS AND TIMING

Access is leverage. Timing is power. Don't be endlessly available. Don't wait too long to act. Windows close.

8. EXPECT THE BACKSLIDE

After boundaries come:
- lovebombing
- fake apologies
- rage
- sudden "commitment"

Plan for it so you don't fold.

9. FIRE VS WATER

Fire ends things. Water delays them.
Distance helps. Removal heals.

10. PAY ATTENTION LIKE A GROWN WOMAN

Watch:
- his environment
- his consistency
- his contradictions
- his reaction to limits
- what survives over time

Patterns don't lie.

140

11. CLEVER MEN BLUR PATTERNS

Confusion is a tactic. Gaslighting scrambles data. Patterns end arguments. Clarity ends games.

12. YOU CAN'T MANIFEST CONSISTENCY

Intuition alerts you. Behavior decides. Vibes are signals. Patterns are proof.

13. RED FLAGS VS TERRAIN

Red flags follow the man. Terrain is context.

You don't need a villain to leave.
You need incompatibility.

14. MOVE ONLY FOR ADVANTAGE

Before you text, explain, confront, or "check in," ask: What do I gain? Relief is not advantage. Clarity, safety, dignity are.

15. NEVER EXIT FOR EGO

Don't leave to punish. Don't block to perform. Exit to protect your future.

16. FEELINGS CHANGE. COSTS DON'T

Loneliness spikes. Nostalgia lies. Time doesn't return. Protect the army. Protect yourself.

FINAL DOCTRINE

You don't need to try harder. You need to see earlier. Strategy is temporary. Peace is the goal. When this works, you won't need it anymore.

THE CLASSICS UNLOCKED COLLECTION

The Classics Unlocked Collection reframes timeless works of philosophy, literature, and strategy through the lens of modern relationships and human behavior. Each volume preserves the original classic text while revealing the hidden psychological insights that still shape how we think, love, and connect today. By bridging ancient wisdom with contemporary dating realities, this series invites readers to rediscover familiar masterpieces as living guides for emotional clarity, self-command, and power in modern relationships.

THE ART OF WAR & DATING

The Art of War & Dating unlocks Sun Tzu's legendary strategies and translates them into the battlefield of modern romance. Through sharp insights and practical reframing, this book explores timing, boundaries, emotional positioning, and strategic awareness in relationships. It is not about manipulation. It is about understanding dynamics, protecting your energy, and learning when to advance, when to wait, and when to walk away with strength.

MEDITATIONS & DATING

Meditations & Dating draws from the private reflections of Roman emperor Marcus Aurelius to offer a grounded, powerful approach to modern relationships. Blending Stoic philosophy with contemporary dating challenges, this book explores emotional discipline, detachment without bitterness, and the quiet confidence that comes from mastering yourself instead of trying to control others. Calm, honest, and deeply human, it is a guide for anyone seeking clarity and peace within the chaos of modern connection.

FROM THE DATING UNEXPERT

I didn't write these books to tell women what to do. I wrote them because I watched too many brilliant women blame themselves for systems that were never built for them to win.

Every book I've written exists for a different moment in a woman's life not to fix her, but to remind her who she already is when she's not apologizing, bargaining, or shrinking to survive.

If this book helped you see more clearly, the others are here to meet you wherever you are next.

THE BREAKUP BAND-AID
(The one that started it all)
This was written for the woman in acute emotional pain. The one who can't sleep, can't eat, can't stop replaying the ending. It doesn't rush healing or romanticize strength. It simply holds you steady while the bleeding slows and reminds you that heartbreak is not a personal failure, it's a human one. This book exists to keep you company in the dark so you don't confuse pain with truth.

THE DATING SURVIVAL BIBLE
This is the field guide. The pattern decoder. The moment you stop asking *"What's wrong with me?"* and start asking *"What keeps repeating and why?"* It's designed to take women out of emotional free-fall and into clarity, discernment, and self-trust. Not rules. Not games. Just reality, clearly labeled.

THE RED FLAG TRANSLATOR

This book exists for the moment your intuition starts whispering but you don't yet trust it. It puts language to what you feel but can't quite articulate: the subtle tells, the phrases that sound harmless but aren't, the behaviors that always lead to the same ending. It's not about suspicion. It's about fluency.

1001 DATING IDEAS

Not every book needs to be heavy. This one is about joy, curiosity, creativity, and remembering that dating doesn't have to feel like a job interview or a trauma reenactment. It's here to reintroduce play, intention, and choice back into connection without abandoning your standards.

BECOMING HER

This book is not about dating at all. It's about identity. It's for the woman who is done centering her life around being chosen and ready to return to herself: her voice, her intuition, her power, her inner coherence. This is the book women read when they stop asking for permission and start living from alignment.

THE ULTIMATE WOMAN'S GUIDE TO LETTING GO

This one is for the season after survival when the noise fades and something quieter, deeper, and more honest begins to emerge. It doesn't force closure. It doesn't rush forgiveness. It teaches release without erasure and helps women put down what they were never meant to carry.

A SINGLE GIRL'S GUIDE SERIES

(Including IVF, sex, and the bucket list)

These books exist to normalize the full, complex, joyful reality of modern womanhood. Desire. Choice. Biology. Humor. Autonomy. They are reminders that there is no single timeline, no single script, and no single way to build a meaningful life. You get to choose and you don't owe anyone an explanation.

AND IF YOU LEARN BEST BY PLAYING...

I've also created games, worksheets, prompts, and tools designed to help you integrate this work into real life not just understand it intellectually. These are for women building businesses, rebuilding confidence, redefining love, or simply learning how to trust themselves again.

You'll find all of that at **yourdatingunexpert.etsy.com**

FINAL WORD

You don't need all of these books.
You don't need to read them in order.
You don't need to become someone else.
You just need the right words at the right moment.

Take what helps. Leave what doesn't. And trust that the version of you this work is pointing toward has been there all along waiting patiently for you to stop abandoning her.

With love,
Your Dating UnExpert